ABOUT THE COVER

That's Mr. Smallmouth to you…
A Fly Anglers Guide for River Smallmouth

This title really does sum up the attitude of the smallmouth bass and it sure embodies their spirit as well. A wonderful game fish, smallmouths are always willing to challenge the angler. They are aggressive when on the feed and readily come to the fly.

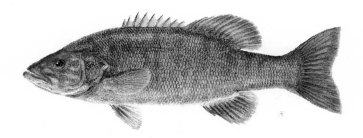

These fish are opportunistic and will eat a variety of food items that they encounter. Smallmouth will take flies throughout the water column and when hooked, fight boldly until brought to hand.

Shortly after their discovery, man recognized the qualities of this fish and began to transport them outside their native region. If not for geographical restraints, there is no doubt that their original range would have been much larger to begin with.

So very adaptable, they have established populations in all the areas where they have been relocated. Bass anglers are very appreciative of this increased range and nowadays consider the smallmouth bass to be one of the best fresh water game fishes available.

Stream notes; Smallmouth, though aggressive feeders, can become very cautious if they sense any danger. A careful approach is recommended especially later in the season or whenever the water is low and clear.

That's Mr. Smallmouth To you...

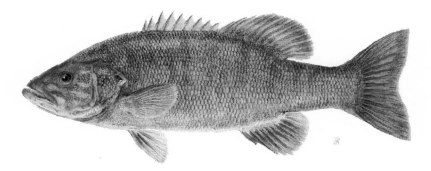

A Fly Anglers Guide
For River Smallmouth

Fly plates photographed by: Beverly Wilkins
Old Hippie Productions Sterling Hts., MI.

Illustrations and photographs created by the author.

CONTENTS

ACKNOWLEDGMENTS

I guess the fish, the smallmouth, have been my most consistent teachers. Studying their reactions to flies, techniques, and methods and making the necessary adjustments has provided an invaluable education. Being absolutely and passionately absorbed in the sport of fly fishing has led me to countless hours wading in streams in pursuit of this incredible game fish. As a result, I have extracted a lot of technical data and gained a great respect for the smallmouth bass. They have never disappointed me with their irrepressible vigor, stamina, and attitude.

To all the other fly fishermen that have interacted with me over the years. Not only on the stream but at all the other functions that tend to congregate people with similar interests.

My children, the two boys and my daughter who occasionally, will take time out from their busy schedules to spend some time fishing with "ole" dad. They always seem to have a compliment or two that makes me feel like I'm the man even though I know that their opinions are biased. And, of course, to my wife Loretta who invariably gave me peace of mind by letting me feel that it was no imposition to her when I suggested going fishing. Remembering that very special day when she allowed me to guide her to her very first smallmouth. Holding that fish up and seeing the grin she had, well, that will always be an inspiration to me.

For a couple of good fishing buddies that over the years rarely refused my invitation to spend time together. For their unwavering patience with me after some of the excursions that I led them on ended up less than successful.

Finally, for all the sportsmen who took the time to write down their experiences so the rest of us can share what they have learned. All this information from books, journals, magazines and papers that is available to the fly angler today is astounding. Over the years; I have accumulated and relied on a lot of this material for guidance. Needless to say, this has been a valuable tool for me as I hope this book will be for others in pursuit of the wily smallmouth

Stream notes; The exchange of information amongst anglers is not only valuable for improved fishing, but also as a way to establish relationships. Long term friendships have been initiated by simply sharing a successful fly pattern on the stream.

The swapping of stories, ideas and perspectives has always enhanced my view of the sport. This holds true on an international level as well. Traveling to foreign countries such as Mexico, Belize, and Japan has given me the opportunity to spend some time with fly fishermen from these places. Even with the language barrier, we were able to communicate because of our deep common interest. The pleasure that is taken from exchanging ideas and little known facts can be addicting and in most cases, very rewarding. It's quite unusual to come away from these encounters without exposure to some new information.

Done for the day.

INTRODUCTION

At the time that I began to fly fish nearly 30 years ago, I was living in the state of Pennsylvania. Near my home were several trout streams and a lot of fly fishermen. Accepting their advice both on and off the stream saved me a lot of learning time. They were willing to share their knowledge and expertise which greatly shortened my journey to becoming a successful fly fisherman. It is my belief that sharing knowledge is a very important aspect of the sport. In recent years when approached by a novice fly fisherman with questions, I've attempted to pass on this philosophy along with the technical information. I hope that this narrative which is an extension of that philosophy will reach even more anglers and help them with their journey to becoming better bass fishermen. Here in South East Michigan where I currently reside, most of my time fishing for smallmouth is on local streams. Fortunately there are a couple of excellent smallmouth rivers close to my home, making it possible for me to visit them frequently during the season.

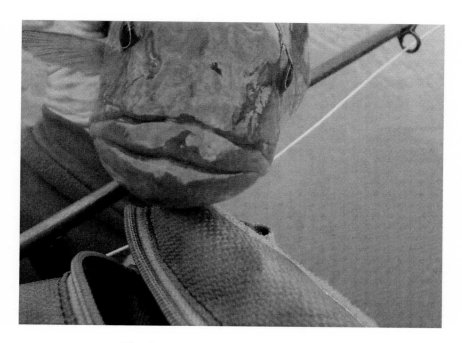

The business end of a smallmouth.

Most of the technical information discussed here was derived through trial and error from many hours on the water. I have attempted to record the techniques, patterns, and methods that have been consistently effective. My intent is that anglers will spend less time on the trial and error part and more time catching fish. Many points will be discussed in these chapters, always interlaced with adaptability and being flexible. Some of the more famous fly fishermen in this country, or in the world for that matter, have based their success on the ability to adjust to the situation at hand. Flexibility will be stressed throughout this book in all aspects of the sport including tying and trying new flies. Proven patterns are very important to all fly fishermen regardless of their skill level, however, I always encourage experimenting with new patterns and ways to fish them. This is an integral part of the sport of fly fishing. After all, even the oldest most celebrated patterns were new at one time! If there is one thing that all anglers will agree on it is that nothing works all the time. Anglers should remain open to changing patterns, methods, or techniques and find the right combination to suit the situation.

Hmmm…let's see, what to use.

Smallmouth are considered a great game fish and deservedly so, as they never fail to excite the angler. I like to think of them as "blue collar fish", not as celebrated as some species but always willing to play their role to complete an enjoyable fishing experience. This is not to say that they are pushovers, not at all. At times, they are just as "picky" as any educated trout but this just adds to their allure. This is especially true if they are spooked or alerted to any danger. They will shut down like any species if they feel threatened. If you experience this, either take a break or move to another spot.

Just a bit more and he's a legitimate catch.

I have had some frustrating days on stream when nothing seemed to work. You have the right position, you throw the right flies, you use the right techniques, and nothing! This scenario has happened to all of us, I'm sure, and it can be discouraging. But, you know, these situations prompt me to try even harder which usually results in something good. Finding a new pattern that works, a better presentation, or maybe some other holding areas in that section of the river are a few of these positive results.

I'd like to share a story with you that changed my perspective on catch and release. Years ago, as a beginning fly fisherman, I was in the habit of harvesting a legal limit of trout every chance that I got. One day when I was wading a favorite section of a local stream, I noticed a fish rising under some low hanging brush. It was tough to get a good drift under there but eventually the fly floated naturally into the feeding lane and disappeared in a swirl. I landed that beautiful 14 inch brown trout, creeled, it took it home and had it for dinner. The next time fishing that section of the stream, I looked over at that low hanging brush and thought about that brown trout. It occurred to me that had I released that fish, I might relive the thrill of getting it to take my fly again. After that day right up to the present, I have rarely harvested a fish of any species. Not to say there is anything wrong with taking fish within the legal limits, that's what the rules are there for. As for me, I prefer to let them swim.

Stream notes; if possible grab the fly and remove it from the fish's mouth. If not, hold the fish by the bottom lip while extracting the fly. Avoid touching the body of the fish as this can remove the protective coating that guards them against contracting diseases.

Like any resource, smallmouth are much too valuable to be left unprotected and without regulations. As anglers, we need to be aware of this and get involved whenever we can to insure their future. A fishery can be decimated, not only from over harvesting but from the destruction of the environment as well. It matters a great deal to practice catch and release and to keep the streams clean. Environmental issues are just as important to the fly fisherman as any technical data.

A lot of fly fishermen, me included, have become a voice for these issues. Being involved has led me to some interesting experiences that have just enhanced my appreciation of the sport. Get involved on your local waters. I'm sure that you will find it a rewarding experience. You know it's the sportsmen that have to pass on the word, especially to the next generation. Eventually, they will have to pick up the flag and carry on. Needless to say, it is imperative that we get them interested and educated in the areas that will preserve our fisheries.

Stream notes; Teaching a kid to appreciate fly fishing at a young age is one of the best insurances we can provide for the sport. Children grasp information so well that they will be very proficient with the fly rod by the time they reach adulthood.

Nice fish, took a stripped nymph.

Hopefully, this guide will be used to generate interest in these issues as well as an instructional tool that actually helps you catch more fish. I will attempt to convey these instructions in such a manner to be easily understood and easy to apply on the stream. With this done, there is no doubt that you will find success in your quest for the Black Bass.

Chapter One

HISTORY

A brief history of the black bass;

A true American, Micropterus Dolomieui, the Black Bass was originally found in most freshwaters of East and Central North America. Back in the day when they were first documented, they were called Black Bass. The word Bass was derived from the old English word "Barse" meaning Perch, but they do not belong to the Perch family. They were then as now, members of the sunfish family The Sunfish family includes Largemouth Bass, Smallmouth Bass, Crappies, Bluegills, Rock Bass, and several other Pan fishes.   Of the eleven or so species in the Black Bass or Sunfish family, the smallmouth will be the focus of this book.

Some common names for this fish in the Midwest are Smallmouth, Smallie, or Bronzeback. Smallmouths are generally brown with dark vertical bands. There are 13-15 soft rays in the dorsal fin. The upper jaw of smallmouth extends to the middle of the eye. The males are relatively smaller than the females.

Males are usually around two pounds while females can range from three to six pounds. Their color will vary from dark brown to a light yellow brown depending on the habitat where they live.

Their scientific classification;

Kingdom: Animilia

Phylum: Chordata

Class: Actinopterygii

Order: Perciformes

Family: Centrarchidae

Genus: Micropterus

Species: M. dolomieu (these last two categories form the Binomial name Micropterus dolomieu) Lacepede, 1802

Smallmouth were native to the upper and middle Mississippi river basin, the Saint Laurence River-Great Lakes system and up into the Hudson Bay Basin. In the United States, the Smallmouth was first moved outside their native range upon construction of the Erie Canal in 1825, extending the fish's range into central New York State. During the mid to late 1800's, Smallmouth were transplanted via the nations rail system to lakes and rivers throughout the northern and Western United States, eventually, getting all the way to California.

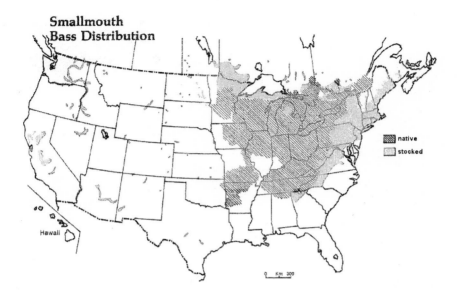

Smallmouth Bass Distribution

As you can see from this illustration, smallmouths have been introduced to many parts of the country and I have no doubt that this hearty fish could survive in a lot of areas not listed here.

The first successful transporting of smallmouth occurred in 1853 after the completion of the Baltimore and Ohio railroad to the Ohio River at Wheeling. The first lot of small fish was placed in a bucket with perforated holes that fit into the opening in the water tank attached to the locomotive. It was supplied with fresh water at the regular water stations along the line and thereby succeeded in keeping the fish alive, fresh, and sound. This lot of fish was put into the basin of the Chesapeake and Ohio Canal from which they could access the Potomac and its tributaries and they survived in grand fashion.

With increased industrialization and development, many of the nation's eastern trout streams were dammed, polluted, deforested, and allowed to silt up raising the water temperature and killing off the native trout.

The smallmouth loves these types of foam bugs.

Smallmouth was introduced into these streams and being hardy and very adaptive, they flourished. Not to say that smallmouth is tolerant of pollution, it's just that they can adjust to changing water conditions better than most trout. There was a time, however, when smallmouth populations began to decline for the same reasons. Man's intervention by building dams, overdevelopment of the land, and the resulting pollution caused such a loss of habitat that their numbers decreased as well. This decline, fortunately, has been reversed in recent years.

Nowadays there is a renewed interest in preserving water quality and natural habitat. This, along with better management practices, has brought a recovery in the smallmouth population.

Stream notes; if pike are intercepting you're smallmouth flies and cutting the line, try going to a heavier tippet, say 15 lb. test especially in the spring when the bass are not leader shy.

It took a while but eventually smallmouths became popular with anglers and are now one of the more sought after freshwater game fishes in the country .Presently, many fly fishermen will list smallmouth as their favorite quarry.

Not an uncommon sight in Michigan Metroparks.

And they are certainly available for today the Black Bass inhabit a distance of more than twenty degrees of latitude or nearly two thousand miles from Florida to Canada. No other game fish in the world has so large a range, solid evidence of their adaptability. Appropriately, more and more fly anglers are discovering the benefits of fishing for this true American, the smallmouth bass.

Giving the fish a rest.

Stream notes; Feeding fish will shut down from too much pressure. Rest the area for awhile, come back later and you will find that the feeding has resumed.

Chapter Two

PHILOSOPHY

For years I have pondered the question: why do fly anglers strive to get the best equipment available? Anyone who has fished for a while knows that inexpensive gear can be just as effective as any in the hands of a skilled fisherman. Of course, there's the durability factor. The better, and usually more costly, gear will generally last longer I suppose for some it's a status symbol but I think most anglers just want to know that they have the best stuff for the job. Still, this wasn't the answer that I was looking for…and then, a couple of years ago in a magazine, there it was; an answer that made sense. It read: *fishermen want the best equipment available because it makes them want to be as good as they can be.* I don't know about you but it works for me. One thing for sure, having the best gear will take away a lot of the excuses.

Most anglers, me included, have experienced what I will call "the evolving fisherman". This is nothing new; it has been written and talked about for many years. I'm mentioning it here because it's exactly what I experienced in my progression from novice to skilled fly fisherman.

At first the novice fly fisherman just wants to catch a fish. Eventually he will want to catch a lot of fish; success will be determined by the number of fish caught. After learning how to take fish consistently, he will begin targeting large fish. Now he wants to catch the largest fish available to him. When he is comfortable with getting large fish regularly, the need to get them the way that he wants becomes the next challenge. It no longer matters how many fish is caught or how big. Now it's just nice to be on the water and getting a fish to take your fly the way that you want is the goal. Getting a large fish to do this is the ultimate goal.

A good explanation of the philosophy of angling was written by Dr. James Henshall in his Book of the Black Bass. This book, published in 1881, was the first definitive work on the black basses. Henshall is considered by some as the father of black bass fishing. Included among the subjects discussed in his book is the smallmouth bass, the main topic of this book.

Some excerpts from Henshalls' book;

Quoting Henshall;

"Why do fish eagerly take bait one day and utterly refuse it the next, when apparently all other conditions are equal? This is a poser and has baffled observant anglers for all ages and will, in all probability, never be solved satisfactorily."

He continues there are many factors that can affect the feeding of fish. With so many variables always present, the fish may react differently depending on what is happening in their environment at a particular time. A bass may be hungry but if he senses danger he probably won't feed even though he did yesterday under the same conditions. The danger could be in the form of an angler, a larger predator fish, a bird flying over casting a shadow, etc. It follows that Henshall and many other anglers agree that keeping out of sight of the fish will increase ones chances for success.

This fish hit a streamer with a crayfish already in its mouth.

Smallmouth rarely roam very far from where they hatched and in their native waters, they are quite timid and ever on the alert for danger. They will not feed if they feel danger and will usually depart the area quickly. I can add this: once these fish are spooked, they become a lot harder to catch. When in the water, wading carefully is always a good idea.

The Black Bass is eminently an American fish and is truly representative in his characteristics. He has the facility of asserting himself and making himself completely at home wherever placed. He is plucky, game, brave, and unyielding to the last when hooked. He has the arrowry rush and vigor of the trout, the untiring strength and bold leap of the salmon, and yet has a system of fighting tactics that are all his own.

Hello baby...

An interesting note from henshall's book:

According to Henshall, the split bamboo fly rod was invented by Samuel Phillippe of Easton, Pennsylvania in the year 1848. Based on his research, Phillippe was the inventor in America and certainly the first in the world to make a four section rod. Those made in England at the time were all three section rods made with three triangular strips glued together. These were known as rent and glued up bamboo rods.

An early Phillippe rod was eleven feet four inches in length and weighed exactly eight ounces. This was a well proportioned rod with the largest swell of butt one inch, inside diameter of the first ferule was 5/16 inch, and the second ferule was 3/16 inch, with the extreme tip down to 3/32 inch. The length of the reel seat was 3 ½ inches with a diameter of 11/16 inch. The length of the butt handle from the reel seat to the end was ten inches including the end cap.

This smallmouth hit just on the edge of those weeds.

The first reported news of a bamboo rod made in England was in 1852. This is what led Henshall to believe Phillippe to be the inventor of the split bamboo fly rod. Samuel Phillippe was born on August 9, 1801 in Reading, Pennsylvania and died in Easton, Pennsylvania on May 27, 1877. Phillippe was a gunsmith by trade.

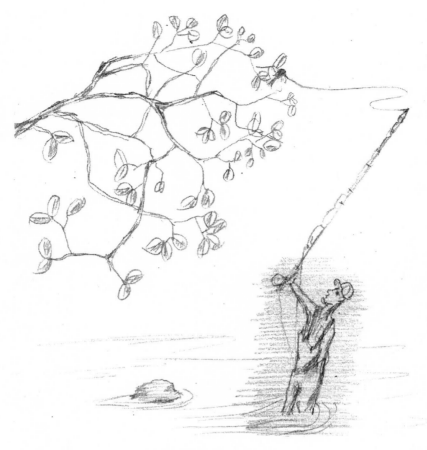

Been there…Done that.

Stream notes; Fly hung up, try a couple of normal tugs on the rod. If this doesn't free the fly, grab the line and pull directly to you. Continued thrashing can result in a broken rod.

A quote from Isaac Walton, possibly the first scholar on fishing;

"The question is not merely to be or not to be, but weather one is capable of learning it, for though anyone may become a bait

fisher, it is not everyone that can learn the fly fishers' art. He that hopes to be a good angler must not only bring an inquiring, searching, and observing wit, but must bring a large measure of hope and patience and a love and propensity to the art itself. Having once got and practiced it, then doubt not but angling will prove to be so pleasant that it will prove to be a reward to itself."

One of my streamer fly boxes.

Another Henshall quote;

"Artificial fly fishing is the most legitimate, artistic, and gentlemanly mode of angling and is to be greatly preferred to all other ways and means of capturing the finny tribe. It requires more address, more skill, and a better knowledge of the habits of the fish and his surroundings than any other method."

It is obvious that Mr. Henshall and Mr. Walton were biased in their opinion of the Black Basses. And I think it is safe to assume they preferred fly fishing to any other method of angling. They tended to be a bit more philosophical in those days, yet their insight into the importance of this game fish for future anglers cannot be denied. All of us that pursue smallmouth today owe these gentlemen a degree of gratitude for promoting the growth of this fishery.

Stream notes; Bug repellants that contain deet are very effective; however, they can be harmful to fly lines. When using these products, avoid contact with anything other than the protected areas.

Chapter Three

FISH FACTS

Smallmouth bass are moderately large robust fish that usually attain a length of more than twelve inches. A twenty inch smallmouth is considered a trophy, especially in river systems. A fish this size will weigh around five pounds. Their color ranges from dark olive brown to pale yellow green with dark vertical bars on the side. The belly is mottled dusky off white which gives it a salt and pepper look. On the head are three or four tiger stripes that radiate from the ear rearward. The eye is usually red or orange. Most rivers are inhabited by several species of fish that are noticeably different in appearance from the smallmouth. The largemouth, however, is real similar in appearance but there are some distinct differences. The body markings are different and of course the mouth of the largemouth extends back beyond the eye, hence the name. With the smallmouth the eye ends just before or right at the eye. This difference is usually how these two fish are distinguished. Also, the dorsal fin of the smallmouth has a very shallow notch.

Smallmouth Bass

Largemouth Bass

In terms of angling for these two fish, there are some common tactics. Both will eat the same flies and both have come to hand in the same stretch of river. In some areas largemouth can provide additional angling opportunities because they will continue to feed even after the water temperature gets above the active limit of the smallmouth. Of the two, I have found smallmouth to be more aggressive especially in moving water or where a current exists.

The young of the smallmouth can be identified by the tri colored tail with the outer most portion edged in white, the middle portion has a black band, and closest to the body an orange color.

Smallmouths are usually found in rocky locations in lakes and streams. In streams they prefer a good percentage of riffles flowing over gravel, boulders, or bedrock. All sunfish are nest builders. The male uses his tail to sweep out a depression in the bottom. He then attracts a female to the nest; sometimes he will even drive her to the nest. After she has spawned, she is driven away from the nest and another female is selected. Often up to three females will lay their eggs in one nest! A female smallmouth produces 2,000 to 7,000 eggs per pound of body weight. The eggs are the adhesive or glutinous type so when the eggs are deposited they fall to the bottom of the nest where they become stuck to the pebbles, etc. All the eggs do not ripen at the same time. They will incubate for two to nine days depending on the water temperature. Weather can play a role in the spawning process as well. Heavy flooding of a stream or river during this time can result in the loss of an entire age class. As fry, if they get swept out into the current, their chances of survival are very slim.

After the female leaves the nest, the male stays and guards the eggs and the resulting fry. While doing this, he becomes very aggressive towards any intrusion of the nest area. Consequently, they are quite vulnerable to anglers at this time. This is why the season remains closed until after the fry have left the nest. Disturbing the males at this point by drawing them off the nest can seriously affect the outcome of the fry. Without the males presence the fry become accessible to predators and there are always predators about. Smallmouth eggs hatch into tiny fish or fry less than 1/5 of an inch long. The fry hide amongst the rocks for a few days living off their yoke sacs before venturing out from the cover. At this time they are totally black hence the name black bass.

Note the light tone of this fish. It will vary depending on the bottom where they live.

Where food is plentiful the young grow rapidly reaching a length of four inches after just a few months. In one year they may reach ten inches, and at two years up to twelve inches in length weighing a pound or more. Even in fertile environments smallmouth require seven to ten years to attain eighteen to twenty inches in length. Smallmouth mature in about three years but continue to grow to their maximum weight of four or five pounds. They can grow even larger in the warmer waters of the southern states where the growing season is extended.

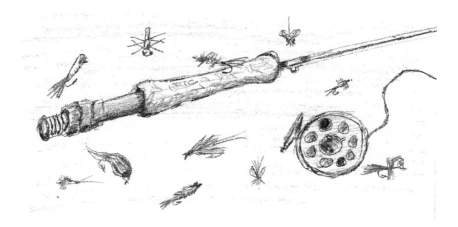

In the colder months of the north, smallmouth that live in streams and rivers become inactive and will retire to wherever they can find seclusion such as deep holes, submerged trees, etc. They will remain dormant until spring when the water temperature gets up over fifty five degrees. Once active, they will feed aggressively.

Smallmouth have a life expectancy of eighteen years, however, only a few ever live half that long. Currently, the largest smallmouth on record weighed eleven pounds fifteen ounces and was twenty seven inches long. It was caught in 1955 from Dale Hollow Lake in Tennessee. The largest recorded smallmouth taken on a fly rod came from Washington's Columbia River in 1966 and tipped the scales at eight pounds twelve ounces.

Fish are cold blooded which means that they adjust their body temperature to the environment. Of course, there are limits to the temperatures they can endure. Smallmouth can function normally in a relatively wide range, however, as the water temperature approaches either limit, the fish will decrease their activity. Generally, seventy degrees is considered ideal for smallmouth although a few degrees in either direction will still find these fish feeding actively. In late summer and early fall as the water cools average size fish will feed less, not so for the larger bass. The big boys feed well into the fall until the water gets down to forty degrees! In fact, this may be the best time to catch the larger smallmouth in the areas where you fish. On my home river in late September and early October is when I might catch several big bass on any given day.

Hatching activity never goes unnoticed.

Smallmouth will readily eat the nymphs or adults of any insect that inhabits their waters. On many occasions I have encountered smallmouth taking insects off the surface during a hatch. And upon producing the correct fly, experienced some wonderful top water action.

Fishing nymphs can be quite deadly in faster water such as riffles and runs where the fish have to commit to the take. Usually, the fish will be near the bottom where the current is slower and it requires less energy to hold while waiting for food. Any dislodged food items will flow down to them just over the bottom so this is where your nymph has to be as well. It should look like a natural that lost its hold and is tumbling downstream.

Casting a nymph into the bank and stripping it out can also be effective.

You know, more anglers are discovering smallmouth fishing all the time. When they become aware of the availability of these

fish, generally in close proximity of their home, they tend to get serious about fishing for them. Most anglers do not live within commuting distance to a trout stream and the occasional trip to these streams does not provide enough fishing time for many of us. To satisfy the urges, we have to rely on warm water fishing closer to home. The smallmouth fills this need admirably.

This may not be a popular theory but I think smallmouth, in terms of feeding, are not so different than trout. It's just that they are a little more aggressive and consequently, a little less cautious.

That first smallmouth, regardless of size, will always be special.

As a result of a deteriorating environment, some trout streams gradually lost their populations of trout due to the resultant rising of the water temperatures and decreased water quality. Enter the smallmouth who flourishes in these conditions. Accordingly, smallmouth fishing has become increasingly more popular.

Here in the Midwest our season runs from April into October depending on the weather and water conditions. This monthly breakdown of activity is what you might expect during a normal season;

April:

Smallmouth bass that reside in lakes begin to enter rivers to spawn. Fishing is good for these bigger bass through the month of May. Anglers target these fish because of their size but it is illegal to harvest them at this time and they must be released to continue their spawning activity. Streamers and nymphs are the best choice of flies for these fish.

Some of my top water flies.

May:

There may be some sporadic surface activity but unless it gets unusually warm, sub surface flies will still be more productive.

June:

As the water warms to over fifty five degrees the fishing gets better all through the river system. Sub surface flies, though still effective, may be substituted with top water stuff at this time.

July:

Smallmouths begin to look up and will readily take surface flies. If you encounter bass chasing minnows near the surface try poppers. They work real well in this situation. Don't abandon streamers that imitate bait fish; they can still be very effective, especially if you get the fly right in where the baitfish is jumping.

August:

August is the prime time of the year to fish top water. The fish are definitely looking to feed on the surface. Poppers, foam bugs, and natural imitations are all good choices in August. Here in Michigan our largest mayfly, the Hexagenia Limbata, hatches in the evenings during this month and can provide some spectacular top water fly fishing.

September:

The fishing may slow a bit but all smallmouths remain active throughout this month. Streamers and nymphs, once again, more often find their way to the end of the angler's line at this time of the year.

October:

Water temperature is the key. As the water cools below the ideal range, sub surface flies pretty much take over. This is a time to try your larger streamers as the big bass will still be on the feed.

The season here in the upper mid west may seem lengthy but anyone who has ever caught these wonderful game fish can tell you, it's not long enough!

Hexagenia duns coming off the river.

Stream notes; In Michigan the smallmouth season opens after their spawning period. This allows them the time necessary to hatch the fry; any spawning male unintentionally caught at this time must be released quickly. He will immediately go back to guarding the nest.

Chapter Four

EQUIPMENT

Although there are many items that can be considered necessary equipment for fly fishing, the following list is what fly fishermen should always have with them for a day of fishing;

Polarized sunglasses, nippers for cutting line, forceps or hemostats, fly box, bug spray, extra leaders, extra tippet material, split shot, strike indicators, a light for fishing after dark, some band aids, water, cap and a license.

This stuff is important for sure, maybe even indispensable in some cases, however, there are just a few tools that are mandatory in order to fly fish. So I will begin with these few basic tools by giving a brief history of them, their descriptions, and the popular choices of anglers today. These five basic implements for fly fishing are the fly rod, the fly reel, a fly line, a leader, and the flies. Most of the information in this chapter will be directed to the beginner fly fisher; however, I'm hoping experienced anglers will benefit from these words as well.

FLY RODS;

The fly rod is perhaps the most recognizable of these tools and for good reason. Aside from its physical presence, it is what propels the fly to the target which is essential to the act of fly fishing. When fly fishing was brought to America by the colonists, it could not have been high on their list of priorities as they struggled to survive in a new world. Eventually fly fishing surfaced and was popularized by some of the more notable sportsmen in American history. Back in those days, the standard material for fly rods was Bamboo. Bamboo reigned for many years as the choice of anglers until sometime in the late forties or early fifties when Fiberglass hit the scene. Fiberglass, though capable in every way, had one overwhelming feature. It was affordable to the masses. It became so popular in all kinds of rod making that Bamboo was all but forgotten. Especially to the angler that wanted to try fly fishing while on a limited budget. Some time later, less expensive Bamboo rods were made available to the public with some success but fiberglass remained more popular.

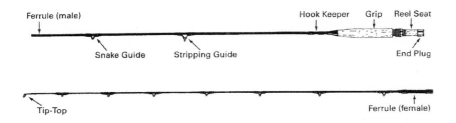

A typical fly rod.

When Graphite came into view it had the same impact that fiberglass had on Bamboo. It virtually took over the market especially for fly rods. Graphite fly rods have continued to evolve through the years into great fishing tools. Modern fly rods are very light, strong, sensitive, and just a joy to use.

Listen up kid, if it smells like bug spray, stay clear

All fly rods, regardless of their construction, are intended to present the fly in such a manner that it looks natural to the fish. Unlike lures, flies are virtually weightless and therefore nearly impossible to cast out with spinning gear. A fly rod accomplishes this by using the weight of the fly line to build energy on the back cast. During the forward cast, the energy is transferred from the rod, through the fly line, down the leader to the fly. In essence it's the weight of the fly line that is cast which is why fly rods are classified by the weight of the line they are designed to throw. The weight or number of the line should match the weight of the rod. This is very important as it enables the rod to load properly so that it casts correctly.

Another important factor is the length of the rod. There are many choices here but most fly rods range from six feet to ten feet long with the more popular length between eight and nine feet.

This dandy came out of the wood in the back ground.

The criteria to consider when choosing a fly rod should include the kind of fish that will be targeted, the type of flies to be used, the size of the water to be fished, and the angler's style of fishing. Of course, sometimes it's just a matter of preference.

Graphite rods were, at first, either made in one solid piece or in two sections. Before long multiple piece rods were available but the first of these seemed heavy in the hand. Eventually, they improved until today, in comparable weights, there is no noticeable difference regardless of the amount of sections! Also, technology and improved manufacturing methods have made them affordable to most anglers and the choice of many fly fishermen.

The action of the rod is another important consideration, how it flexes under pressure. Modern rods have either a slow, medium, or fast action. A slow action rod will bend all the way down to the handle. A medium action rod loads from the middle and a fast action rod uses just the top one third of the rod length. Slow action rods are generally used for closer fishing where a delicate presentation is necessary. Faster rods are needed to get more line out for longer casts. Most anglers today opt for the medium action which is more forgiving of casting errors yet still having the power to get the fly out there.

For the traveling angler multiple section rods have become indispensable as they will fit into luggage and some will even fit into a briefcase! There are so many good rods today that it would be impractical to list them all and they are available in all price ranges. Those anglers on a limited budget can still get a quality rod. Most buy the best that they can afford in a rod that will suit their needs, usually dictated by the species of fish or the type of water to be fished.

A popular choice for river Smallmouth is either a five or six weight medium action graphite rod between eight and nine feet long. The fly rod is probably the most recognized component in the fly fishing arsenal and I think you will agree that it truly symbolizes the sport.

REELS;

Reels for fly fishing are another important tool in the fly fisherman's arsenal. Like the rods, reels have evolved down through the years into very sophisticated pieces of equipment. Yet their function has pretty much remained unchanged, that is to store the line when it's not in use. Those first reels were the single action type meaning one revolution of the handle winds in one turn of line. Many different reels have been invented since then and some are widely used, however, the single action remains the most popular. It is quite adequate for smallmouth fishing. These early reels had an exposed rim that enabled anglers to "palm" the rim with their hand to provide drag or tension to slow the fish down. Although this feature still exists on modern reels, most anglers prefer reels with a built in drag system. The drag is used to keep tension on the line especially when playing a fish. This really helps tire the fish quickly which is conducive to catch and release. The new drag designs are perhaps the most important feature on the reels today. Increasing the diameter and the width of the arbor by creating large arbor reels has also had a profound effect on the modern reel. This enables the line to spool quicker per revolution of the handle. This is desirable on reels used for big game where getting them on the reel as soon as possible is critical to landing the fish.

Giving advice or taking lessons....looks like a good cast either way.

Just about all reels today have extra spools available for all their models. With an additional spool you can change to a different line right on stream to meet the conditions. Also, this enables the angler to use the same reel for two or three rods by simply using the spool with the matching line size.

Almost all reels are made from an aluminum alloy. Some are cast in a mold and others are machined. The machined reels usually cost more because of the labor involved to make them but they are precisely made and will remain relatively maintenance free for many years. There is wide variety to pick from; each designed to handle two or three line sizes. As previously stated, any single action reel is adequate for smallmouth. They don't make the long screaming runs that go into the backing. The majority of the fish caught will be in the one to two pound range. These are easily handled by reels without an inexpensive drag system. When buying a reel, my advice is to get the best that you can afford. The extra cost is usually reflected in a better design that equates to a trouble free reel.

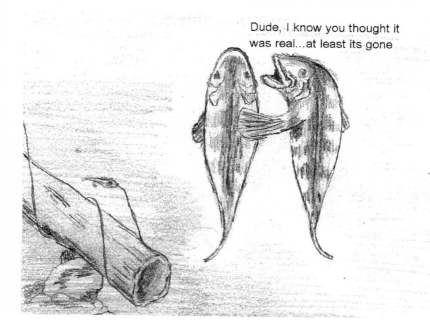

FLY LINES;

Fly lines have come a long way since the days when they were made of horsehair. These first lines required a lot of maintenance to keep them buoyant. And they were not very durable. Technology has changed lines so much that today they are becoming engineering wonders. Some are designed to float; others are intended to sink at varying rates to suit different conditions. There is floating weight forward, floating double taper, floating level, intermediate, sink tip, and full sink lines. All are very durable and have slick finishes that allow for effortless movement through the guides. Modern fly lines are made for specific purposes and methods of fishing. They have many weight classes with the weight placed in different areas of the line depending on its intended use. The weighted areas are just sections with a larger diameter that creates the added weight. The amount of increase in diameter, the length and location of the larger section, and the transition areas back down to the original line diameter are the variables needed to dedicate a fly line for a specific use.

Reel end 80'   60'   40'   20'

LEVEL LINE (L)

WEIGHT FORWARD (WF)

DOUBLE TAPER (DT)

Popular fly line designs.

34

The majority of anglers today use a weight forward line, the weight or heavier section is near the end that attaches to the leader. This lets the line shoot out with less effort and usually results in a more accurate cast when some distance is needed. Double taper lines are normally used for in close fishing where a delicate presentation is required with the weight located in the middle of the line. This line is more economical because both ends are tapered so that when one end wears out you swap to the unused end, however, the distance in your casting will be sacrificed. Floating lines add the versatility of fishing top water or adding some weight to the tippet, say in the form of a split shot, and fishing sub surface. Most anglers opt for this rather than change to a different line.

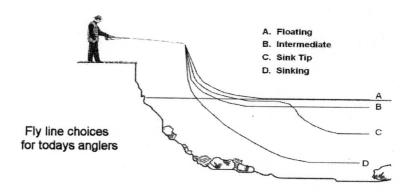

A. Floating
B. Intermediate
C. Sink Tip
D. Sinking

Fly line choices
for todays anglers

Intermediate lines have varying sink rates for under water fishing where the water is fairly shallow. A sink tip line can be used for this as well. The tip of the line is weighted to get it down without the need for additional weight. Some anglers prefer this line because they do not have to deal with split shot hanging up on the bottom. These two sinking lines are commonly used in streams and rivers where the water is moving. There are other lines on the market but these mentioned are normally used for bass fishing, especially when there is a current. Selecting the correct weight line for your rod is mandatory! The correct weight is necessary to load the rod sufficiently on the back cast so the energy from the rod will lay the line out on the forward cast. Some anglers will use one line size larger to aid in the casting by loading the rod even faster. All the new lines work well and are available in a wide range of prices. The better ones are pricey because of the technology built into them due to the research time needed to refine the product to create the desirable characteristics that today's fly fishermen demand.

LEADERS;

A leader plays a substantial role in the fly fishing system, having three basic functions. It provides an invisible connection between the fly line and the fly, it helps to present the fly correctly, and it allows the fly to respond to the current flows in a lifelike manner. This transference of energy is accomplished because leaders have a continuous taper from the fly line where it is attached, down to the tippet that holds the fly. The size of the tippet is determined by the size of the fly to be used. This smooth transfer of energy allows the fly to be presented in a natural manner.

Stream notes; Try using a small swivel in your leader system to eliminate line twist.

Landing a nice smallie in the magic hour on a summer evening,

Modern leaders evolved in the late 1940's. Before then they were made from drawn silkworm gut. Level pieces of gut were joined with knots to form a tapered leader. But gut is brittle unless soaked in water for a few hours and it mildews and rots if not carefully dried when put away. Needless to say, this was a lot of work for anglers so when the use of nylon surfaced, it was a welcome change. Modern leaders are made from polymer materials such as nylon, monofilament or fluorocarbon.

Generally, leaders are 60% butt section, 20% mid section, and 20% tippet in reference to the overall length. The butt section is made of somewhat stiffer material than the other sections to help transfer the energy the mid and tippet sections need to be softer to allow natural movement of the fly. These sectional figures are just a guide and it is not uncommon for leaders to vary, especially those developed for a specific purpose. Leaders can be tapered continuously or they can be made in sections that are attached with knots. Both styles are widely used today. The knotted leaders, the ones that are made in sections, lend themselves to specific formulas so they can be custom made for given situations. A famous fly fisherman, Mr. George Harvey, took building leaders to another level, maybe even approaching a science! He was a pioneer and an ambassador for the sport of fly fishing in many areas. Those of us that began to fly fish in the state of Pennsylvania quickly learned the benefits of his leader formulas. Perhaps even more importantly, we found that building leaders for certain kinds of fishing could improve the presentation of the fly and ultimately, increase the catch ratio.

Building a leader is not a complicated endeavor, in fact, it's pretty easy.

You're not from around here, are you?

Wow! What a beauty, this fish gave it up to a crayfish pattern.

Smallmouths are not very leader shy so the leaders used for them can be fairly simple and not so long. In fact, some anglers use just straight mono but I think a tapered leader is more effective. Two common lengths for smallmouth are 7 ½ and 9 feet; however, a longer leader may be useful when fishing on top in low and clear water. I recommend using as short a leader as you can without hampering the action of the fly. These two lengths are always found in retail stores and of the two, the 7 ½ footer is quite adequate for most bass fishing.

Another factor to consider for leaders is the size of their tippet end or the end that attaches to the fly. They are given an "x" number which determines the size of the tippet and references to the pound test of the line. Usually a 2x will test out at about 8 pounds, 3x at 6 pounds, 4x at four pounds, etc. These values may vary from one manufacturer to another but not too much. All the current brands are pretty consistent. So if you are targeting a fish that requires 8 pound test, use a leader that has this rating, usually it will be a 2x or 3x. As you continually change flies with a tapered leader, the diameter will get larger. Assuming that you are using the same size fly, it will become increasingly harder to lay the fly out there correctly. To avoid this, I tie a loop at the end of the leader after a few fly changes. To this loop attach a length of tippet material the same size as the original tippet. When this gets too short, simply replace it with it with another piece. With this method you may not have to change leaders all day! Most fly fishermen carry two or three spools of tippet material in the sizes needed for that day of fishing.

Another item that I sometimes use on my bass leaders is a small swivel (preferably size 18). It may be uncommon to add any weight like this to a leader but adding this small amount dose not affect the performance of the leader when fishing for bass. You can attach the swivel anywhere in the system. I usually attach mine between the butt and mid sections or in the case of knotless leader, between the leader and the tippet. This effectively removes a lot of the leader twist associated with throwing air resistant flies such as poppers and foam bugs. The flies will land on the water correctly, they will float better and they will appear more natural to the fish.

A well placed cast into that foam prompted this guy to take.

Here are some standard leader formulas:

7 ½ foot leaders;

0X

24" of .019, 16" of .017, 14" of .015, 9" of .013, 9" of .012, 18" of .011

1X

24" of .019, 16" of .017, 14" of .015, 9" of .013, 9" of .011, 18" of .010

2X

24' of .019, 16" of .017, 14" of .015, 9" of .013, 9" of .011, 18" of .009

3X

24" of .019, 16" of .017, 14" of .015, 6" of .013, 6" of .011, 18" of .008

4X

24" of .019, 16" of .017, 14" of .015, 6" of .013, 6" of .011, 18" of .007

9 foot leaders;

0X

36" of .021, 16" of .019, 12" of .017, 8" of .015, 8" of .013, 8" of .012, 20" of .011

1X

36" of .021, 16" of .019, 12" of .017, 8" of .015, 8" of .013, 8" of .012, 20" of .010

2X

36' of .021, 16" of .019, 12" of .017, 8" of .015, 8" of .013, 8" of .011, 20" of .009

3X

36" of .021, 16" of .019, 12" of .017, 6' of .015, 6" of .013, 6" of .011, 6" of .009,20" of .008

4X

36" of .021, 16" of .019, 12" of .017, 6' of .015, 6" of .013, 6" of .011, 6" of .009, 20" of .007

5X

28" of .021, 14" of .019, 12" of .017, 10" of .015, 6" of .013, 6" of .011, 6" .009, 6" of .007, 20" of .006

Common Tippet sizes

0X...............011" diameter...............13 pound test

1X...............010" diameter...............11 pound test

2X...............009" diameter...............9 pound test

3X...............008" diameter...............6.5 pound test

4X...............007" diameter...............5.5 pound test

5X ....006" diameter...............4.5 pound test

6X...............005" diameter............... 3.5 pound test

7X...............004" diameter...............2.5 pound test

8X...............003" diameter...............1.75 pound test

They sure like this leech pattern.

There are many leaders available, experiment until you find what works best for your style of fishing. If you take the time to get the right leader, your casting will improve and you will present the fly more effectively. On occasion I will purchase knotless leaders and they work just fine but normally, I build my own. Its fun to experiment with different formulas, you know, always looking for a little better combination. You can buy spools of monofilament line in different sizes and make leaders as you need them. The sections are connected with a blood knot. Blood knots can be tied by hand but there are tools available that make this chore real easy. The down side to knotted leaders is that the knots do catch flotsam occasionally but I think the advantage of customizing a leader to suit your needs out weighs this. I'm including the formulas to a few leaders that I use regularly. Keep in mind that these formulas are for more delicate presentations usually associated with fishing top water especially if you are attempting to match a hatch. If you decide to build your own leaders, regardless of the formula, just make sure that each section gets progressively smaller in diameter and shorter in length. Usually each section will drop about five pounds in strength which equates to only a difference of .002 or .003 per inch. The exception to this is the tippet section, though still smaller in diameter, will be longer than the previous section to allow natural movement of the fly.

Bluegills on the fly…This is how it all starts.

Following are my leader formulas along with illustrations that show the basic connections in a typical arrangement, how these knots are tied, and the loop to loop system.

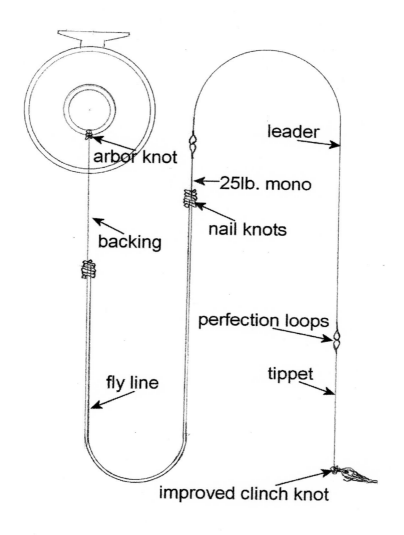

arbor knot

backing

fly line

leader

25lb. mono

nail knots

perfection loops

tippet

improved clinch knot

Basic Connections

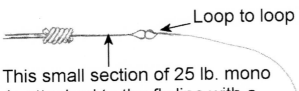

Loop to loop

This small section of 25 lb. mono
is attached to the fly line with a
nail knot. It stays with the fly line
and facilatates changing leaders
using the loop to loop method.

butt
section

blood knots

A TYPICAL LEADER

mid
section

This shows a typical
leader assembled with
a butt section of two
segments, a mid section
of two segments and
a tippet section.

tippet

Here are the formulas to the leaders that I use regularly;

1. A good leader for larger flies   7 feet – 3X
    24" of 25 pound test
    16" of 20 pound test
    12" of 15 pound test
    8" of 10 pound test
    24" of 6 pound test tippet

2. A good choice for streamers   71/2 feet – 3X
    24" of 25 pound test
    18" of 20 pound test
    14' of 15 pound test
    10' of 10 pound test
    24" of 6 pound test tippet

3. A good general purpose leader   9 feet – 3X
    30' of 25 pound test
    24' of 20 pound test
    18' of 15 pound test
    12" of 10 pound test
    24" of 6 pound test tippet

4. Real good for all around top water   81/2 feet – 4X
    24" of 25 pound test
    20" of 20 pound test
    16' of 15 pound test
    12" of 10 pound test
    8" of 6 pound test
    24" of 4 pound test tippet

5. Good for top water when low and clear   10 feet – 4X

    36" of 25 pound test

    24" of 20 pound test

    18" of 15 pound test

    12" of 10 pound test

    6" of 6 pound test

    24" of 4 pound test tippet

Hellgrammites, when available, are readily eaten by smallmouth.

Here are the knots needed for these leader systems;

Arbor Knot

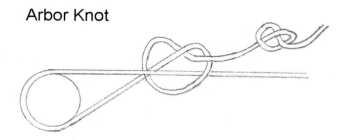

This knot is used to connect the backing to the reel. Just loop the line around the arbor of the spool and tie in two overhand knots. The outside know simple prevents the line from slipping through when pulling the line tight around the arbor. Tighten the outside knot, then the inside knot and pull on the standing line. Although the knots are tight, the loop will tighten onto the arbor.

Nail Knot

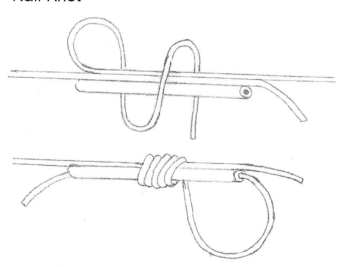

Overlap enough of the leader to make the wraps. Holding the tube, fly line, and the leader, wrap the tag end of the leader five times. With the wraps snug, insert the tag end into the tube. Push through so that it exits the other end. Pinch down over the wraps and remove the tube. Slowly pull the tagged end of the leader and the standing line at the same time. Be sure that the fly line is outside the knot and keep the wraps together when tightening.

Loop To Loop

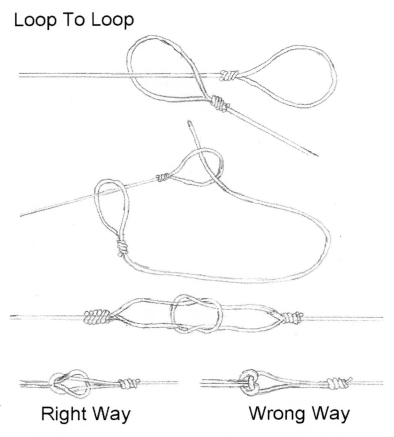

Right Way   Wrong Way

Here are two perfection loops used to connect the fly line to the leader to the tippet. This arrangement is a quick way to change these components.

Perfection Knot

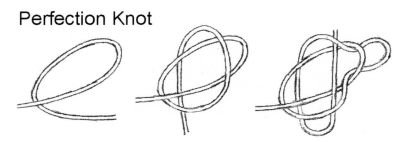

I like this knot because it has nearly 100% knot strength and the loop finishes straight, not leaning to one side.

Blood Knot

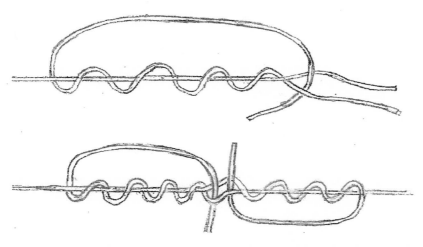

Overlap the lines by a sufficient amount. Wrap five times on one side and pull the end through between the two lines. Repeat on the other side, pulling the end through the lines in the opposite direction. Hold the two tag ends as you gather the knot. When this done pull on the lines to tighten the knot. This is the knot for building the body of the leaders.

Improved Clinch Knot

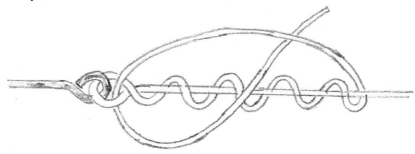

Insert the tippet through the eye of the hook. Wrap at least five times around the standing tippet line. Then insert the tag end back through the original loop and slowly pull the knot tight. Hold the tag end while pulling on the standing line.

Non Slip Knot

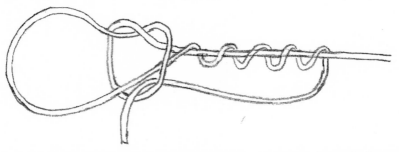

Tie a simple overhand knot then bring the tag end back through the loop. Wrap around the standing line and back through the loop. The amount of wraps on the standing line depends on the size of the line. 3X requires seven wraps, 2X five, and so on. Pull the tag until the knot forms then pull both the tag and the standing line until tight. This knot could be used when you want the fly to move freely and without restriction.

Rapala Loop Knot

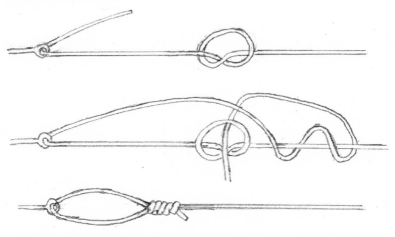

Tie an overhand knot with at least three inches of tag end. Put the tag end through the eye of the hook. Take it back past the overhand knot, wrap three times around the standing line, then go back through the overhand knot. Pull tight while taking note the size of the loop.

TECHNIQUES

Having all the right tools and information won't help you catch
fish unless you apply them correctly by using some proven
techniques. I'm sure that there are effective techniques that
aren't listed here but these are some that I have found to be
consistently successful. They will be discussed in the order that
you would need them in a normal day of fishing. Of course,
there are some factors that will always affect the fishing
regardless of where and how you fish. These are water clarity,
temperature of the water, the time of the day, and the time of the
year. Just remember that these factors can and usually do
impact the information that we will discuss in this chapter.
Varying conditions, usually created by the weather, will always
influence what smallmouth will eat on any given day .When it's
raining, for example, forget about top water and go under with
nymphs or streamers. Unlike largemouth, smallmouths are
reluctant to rise when it's raining. Also, they are slow to come up

until the water warms sufficiently. Surface fishing is normally associated with low and clear water but this is not always the case. In early spring rivers are usually running high, however, if you find them low and clear surface fishing might not be good because of the water temperature. It may still be too cool for the fish to feed actively. Conversely, later in the season when the water temperature is adequate, you can catch Smallmouth on top even if the water is high and off color! So water temperature is real important, especially during the transitional periods between the seasons.

Good fishermen are adaptable and the successful angler should be flexible and change flies, methods, and sometimes even equipment to suit the conditions. You have to determine what the fish are eating and hopefully have the flies needed to fool them. Usually, a smallmouth's diet will include insects, crayfish, leeches, and minnows or smaller fish. These food items are real important to the fly fisherman because he will have to imitate them to attract the fish.

The author with a nice smallmouth taken on a Silver Streak

Let's begin with your arrival at the stream. One of the most important techniques is learning to read the water. Reading the water will help you locate any fish in the area. As you approach the water where you plan to fish there are several items to consider. Stop and survey the scene, taking a few minutes to focus on what is happening can really be helpful. Look for any insect activity, any bugs coming off the water or flying around. Check to see if there is any structure that could hold fish such as rocks, deadfalls, weed beds, ledges, undercut banks, or logjams. Are there any current seams where slower and faster water meet, usually caused by some form of structure. Smallmouths prefer to hang around structure such as those previously mentioned. These structures are all prime holding areas. Like most fish, smallmouths want to be near a food source with access to cover. When you encounter a current seam near cover, this is definitely a prime holding area. Current seams create feeding lanes that usually hold some fish. Smallmouth will sit in the slower water and dart out for any food items that come by, and then return to the safety of the cover. Be sure to fish the edge of the seam that is adjacent to the slower water, this is a great spot to get a fish. On bright, sunny days you will want to be more careful when approaching the good fishing areas. If the fish sense any danger they will be a lot tougher to catch so move slow and deliberately.

14 inches of bronze, a nice fish, especially on top water!

You may want to check the temperature of the water, 60 degrees or higher should find the fish looking up and they might take flies off the surface. How is the clarity of the water in terms of the distance the fish can see, smallmouth are sight feeders. Position yourself so that you can effectively cover this water. You don't have to be a champion caster to be successful at bass fishing; however, a good presentation will require that you get within your casting distance of the target area.

This won't require long hauls because most smallmouths are caught relatively close to the angler. Without getting too deep into the mechanics of fly casting, I'd like to mention a couple of basic steps that should help with your presentation. In my opinion, two important aspects of fly casting are to find the rhythm of the rod and timing the casting stroke. If the rod has a slow action, slow down your arm movements accordingly. Also, you must stop the arm movement on the backstroke to allow the line to load the rod. Most anglers stop around 12 noon or one o'clock. Wait until you feel the line pulling on the rod, then start the forward stroke. Again, coordinate the arm speed to the action of the rod. Like anything else, casting a fly well takes some practice. Anyone new to the sport would do well to solicit some pointers from those that have the expertise to instruct. It makes sense to learn the correct way prior to developing bad habits.

Wading stealthily, making a good cast, using the right fly, are all important to be sure but learning to read the water will be perhaps the most useful skill one can attain. Knowing where the fish are is the key factor in determining how to use the other skills mentioned.

Moving a little upstream or down stream, adding or removing weight are other factors that will affect the presentation. This is why reading the water is so important. Knowing where the fish should be will enable you to take the best shot at getting any fish that are holding there. Let's back up a bit too when you first looked at this section of the stream. We will assume that you have determined the best water was on the other side near the far bank. Resist wading right over there, instead, fish you way over. Again, if conditions are right, smallmouth can be anywhere in the stream especially if there is some form of structure.

Good fishermen do their homework and will know what food items should available in the area they are fishing. Are there any insects present and if so, have the respective flies for them. For example, damselflies may be hovering just above the surface of the water sometimes alighting for a couple of seconds. Be assured, the bass see this and may rise to take them during this brief period. The rise will be a couple of rings expanding out from the point of the take, usually there will be some bubbles within the circle. The bubbles verify that the bug was taken off the surface upon seeing this, put on a floating damsel pattern and get it on the water just upstream from where the rise was. It's important to know that the quicker you get your fly there, after the rise, the better the chance of getting that fish. No take....try a different pattern but stay with this approach.

Most fly fishermen that target smallmouth have more than one pattern for any given situation, any of which could work. If you are intent on fishing top water try these different patterns especially if they are new. Do not be afraid to experiment, who knows, you may discover a "go to" fly that will become a regular in your arsenal. Of course presentation is always important. A lot of bugs hatch in relatively shallow, moving water. If you cannot get a drag free drift over the target area because of the current, adjust your cast or slowly move to a better position. The fly must look like a natural floating on the surface.

When the fish are feeding on a hatching insect regardless of the species they will probably refuse anything that doesn't resemble the natural. Catch one if you can because they will look a lot different up close than when they are flying. You want to match these bugs, especially the size. The size is the more important feature with general characteristics being second.

Caddis

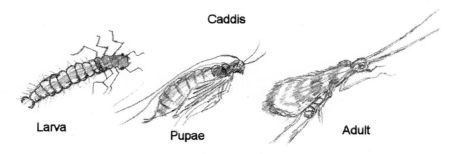

Larva

Pupae

Adult

Another form of rise is when the fish are propelling themselves out of the water. These fish are chasing emergers which are insects swimming to the surface to hatch. When an insect reaches its time to go, it makes a break for the surface in a hurry.

If this activity is spotted, the fish has to move fast to catch the bug, usually just below the surface with its momentum carrying it out of the water. In this scenario the fish will ignore top water flies so go under with nymphs or wet flies that imitate the hatching activity. In the case of a mayfly or a caddis, I would change to the nymph pattern for the fly and float it dead drift on the surface. With this method the fly must stay on top so add some floatant if necessary.

Ah the river in summer…can you tell that he loves his job.

In most cases (but not always) when fishing emergers, there is no need for weight. Cast the fly out and across, strip it under and let it swing. No action…..at the end of the swing, retrieve in short jerks to simulate the bug struggling to get to the surface. If this procedure is not working, add a little weight so that the fly gets closer to the bottom especially in deeper or faster water. The fish will be looking for food somewhere in the water column, you need to find where that is! Wet flies are not as popular as other types but a lot of times they are actually more effective! Since wet flies are moving rather quickly when eaten by a fish, the fish have to commit and the takes are solid and unmistaken. Wet flies have saved many a day for me.

Regardless of how you are fishing, on top or under, remember to try something different. This can be tough to do if you are hitting fish regularly but necessary if you want to find new flies that work. If you experience a situation where everything is working, the fly is good, the presentation is right, and you are consistently taking fish. This may be a time to try some different flies, be sure to present them in the same way as the others so the only variable is the fly.

We know there are several food items in any river system for smallmouth to eat; insects are just one of them. Crayfish are a favorite food source for smallmouth because they have a similar habitat. These crustaceans live around pebbles, stones, and rocks that they need for protection from predators. When searching for food crayfish will move around rather slowly on their legs. If disturbed, however, they can propel themselves backwards very quickly with just a flick of their tail as they head for the nearest cover. In our area, crayfish grow to a final length of around four inches and they will molt or shed their skin several times. During these periods they tend to be lighter in color with a softer body and are particularly desirable to smallmouth, especially when they are in the one and one half to two inch range.

If you tie your own flies, try a lighter shade on the crayfish patterns and if you like to add pinchers, keep them small. Smaller claws are less intimidating to the fish. When fishing a crayfish fly, stay close to the bottom and apply a jigging action if possible. Just about always, when there are juvenile crayfish available, smallmouth will focus on them instead of other food items in the area. Finding or developing a good crayfish pattern will really increase any smallmouth angler's success rate.

Leeches are available in most rivers and streams and provide another common food source for smallmouths. Any dark, narrow, and flowing fly can be effective as a leech pattern. Condensing the equipment needed for a days fishing has been a passion of mine. In warm weather that includes fishing in just shorts. On rare occasion, I have come out of the water with a leech attached, usually somewhere on the lower leg. Not a pleasant experience for sure, however, this does afford the opportunity to observe this creature up close. They have a relatively small cylindrical body tapering down from the head to the tail. They appear to be dark brown or black in color and are usually less than two inches long. Leech patterns can be just as simple. I have some jazzed up patterns that work well but a single strip of rabbit tied onto the hook can be just as effective. When they swim they have a wiggle motion and this is the action that you want to imitate with your fly.

Leech flies are fished like streamers. They can be cast up stream and allowed to swim down with the current or over and across and stripped back. Remember to jiggle the rod now and then to add that wiggle to the fly. If a fish is following the fly, the wiggle sometimes provokes the strike. Leeches like to hang around weed beds so get the fly in as close as possible to the edge of the weeds.

Don't ignore any pockets of water that are surrounded by weeds. These are excellent holding areas for smallmouth. First, work the outside of the weed line adjacent to the main stream. Then cast over the weeds into the pocket. If the pocket is large enough, move into the inside edge and fish the area from there. These areas usually have some shallow water where you can see the bottom, especially on sunny days. The fish can be in these areas but will most likely hold in any darker water that might be created by either shade or depth. The darker spots are your target areas. As always, fish the water closest to you first and gradually increase the distance. Sight fishing or fishing to fish that you can see is exciting but not seeing the fish does not mean that they are not there. Smallmouth blend in real well with their environment and unless they move, can be hard to detect.

Minnows, or small baitfish, are without doubt the most imitated food source for predator fish and for good reason, they constitute a major portion of their diet. Fishing streamer flies that are tied to imitate this baitfish can be considered a "go to" method. By this I mean, when the fishing gets slow, put on a streamer. Streamers in the form of minnows, leeches, or crayfish will almost always generate some action.

Minnows only move when they have to and then their movements are quick and jerky. This is why the "twitching" method works so well, it simulates this movement.

A good fish, typical of this river system, decided to eat a white streamer.

Twitching the fly, sometimes even radically, can bring savage strikes. I have had smallmouth, good size smallmouths, come ten feet to hit a twitched streamer in clear water. Most of my streamers are tied with weighted eyes. This is usually an adequate amount of weight for smallmouths especially when the water gets low, however, weight can be added if necessary in deeper water.

When fishing a streamer or a nymph in skinny water, cast as close to the bank as possible. Let the fly sink for just second before beginning the retrieve. A lot of the time a fish will take right then, especially if it is a good size fish. The bigger fish don't wait around. They will grab the fly sometimes as soon as it hits the water. If this does not happen, keep the fly coming as the smaller fish will follow for a while before taking. In deeper water, particularly if there is a current, you may have to add some weight to get the fly down. Another way to accomplish this is to mend the line. Mending is rolling or looping the line upstream once or twice after the cast. This procedure will slow the drift enough to allow the fly to sink. Mending can also be applied to fishing top water. We will discuss this a little later in the chapter. The depth of the water and the current speed will dictate how aggressively you will have to mend to get the fly down in front of the fish. The point is that you must get the fly to the fish regardless of where they are in the water column. Never assume that there are no fish in front of you. It's better to assume that your presentation is not correct!

Like all flies, streamers can be tied in either a realistic or an impressionistic style. I have found the latter to be more effective. Impressionistic flies are not exact copies of a food source but instead they resemble them enough to draw strikes. These streamers are tied with materials that give them an enticing motion and some flash for attraction. Adding eyes in the form of dumbbell, bead chain, plastic, or machined brass is another feature that can increase the productivity of the fly.

Successful anglers are always adjusting the depth of the fly to suit the water they are fishing usually by changing the amount of weight. Always start with as little weight as necessary and add until you either hit a fish or begin hanging up on the bottom. Another advantage to fishing streamers is they give the angler the ability to cover a lot of water. You can cast across and bring the fly right back or allow it to swing down with the current, sometimes letting the fly hang downstream for a bit. Other times, I will cast upstream and swim the fly down with the current. With this last technique, adding a "popping" action really entices the fish and helps keep the fly from hanging up on the bottom.

Nymph fishing can always be productive but is best in moving water that is relatively shallow. A couple of good reasons; insects usually hatch in this type of water and because of the current; the fish have to commit to the take. Nymph patterns are intended to imitate insects that live on the bottom of a stream. At times they lose their hold and are swept downstream making them accessible to the fish. Any dislodged insect drifting down is moving rather quickly and if a fish decides to eat the bug, has to get on it fast! This can, but not always, creates enough of a disturbance in the drift to alert the angler of the take. Duplicating this scenario with a fly is called dead drift nymphing. The fly must tumble downstream with the current in a natural manner. Any irregular movement by the fly will alert the fish that something is wrong and will result in a refusal. When a good drift is accomplished, it can be difficult to perceive the take should the fish grab the fly. A fish can pick up the fly, mouth it, and expel it without the angler knowing it! At best, there will be a slight hesitation and this pause is what the angler needs to notice to know when to set the hook. Perceiving the take is what makes nymphing so difficult and why a tight line is necessary. Its no wonder that dead drift nymphing is considered by many to be one of the hardest tactics to master. Once learned, however, it can be a very effective way to take fish.

The term "high sticking" is the name given to this method of nymph fishing because this technique keeps as much line as possible off the water. The less line between the fly and the angler improves the response time if the angler perceives a take. The rod is kept high with sometimes just the leader in the water as the rod follows the drift downstream. Be cautious, however, not to impart any unnatural action to the fly. Use enough line and leader to get the fly down and drifting naturally. Any hesitation should be acted upon by lifting the rod slightly. If it is a fish you will feel it immediately. With this method it is crucial to get the fly as close to the bottom as possible without hanging up. You should feel the weight or the fly "ticking" off the bottom, if not, add weight till you do. When mastered, this technique is a deadly way to take most species of fish.

Stream notes; some anglers add weight to the flies instead of the line and if they tie, will use a particular color thread so they know that the fly is weighted.

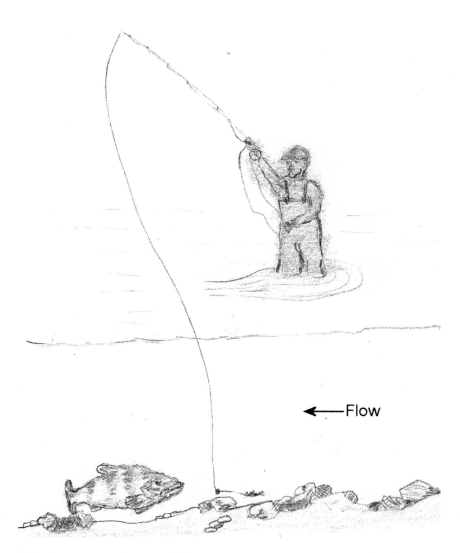

←——Flow

When nymphing for smallmouth and you encounter an abrupt change in the bottom or even a noticeable depression, chances are there will be a couple of fish there. Catching these fish will require getting the fly down to them. If you have drifted through the target area with no results, it's probably because the fly isn't down! When the current is moderate, just cast a little farther upstream. This will give the fly more time to get deeper. Still no results, add some weight in the form of split shot until you feel the shot "ticking" the bottom as the fly drifts down with the current. After adding the weight the cast can be closer to the target area, in fact, keep your cast as close to the fish as possible without spooking them. Cast and drop the rod to let the fly sweep down quickly to the fish. Either way, follow the drift down with the rod keeping as much line off the water as possible without hampering the movement of the fly. If all these factors are applied and the presentation is good with no action, try a different fly before moving on.

Those fly fishermen who become good at nymph fishing develop a sense for anticipating the take. The only way to get this sense is to spend a lot of time on the water practicing. Using strike indicators is another method to help increase your catch rate when nymphing. Strike indicators make it easier to detect any change in the movement of the leader or the line. Indicators are attached to the leader at a distance so the fly will be just off the bottom. They are adjusted to suit the changing water depths. The indicator should float at the same speed or slower than everything else on the surface.

Stream notes: indicators are especially helpful when fishing long deep pools. With a little mending it's possible to keep the fly in the strike zone for much of the pool, thereby keeping the fly in front of the fish for a longer period of time.

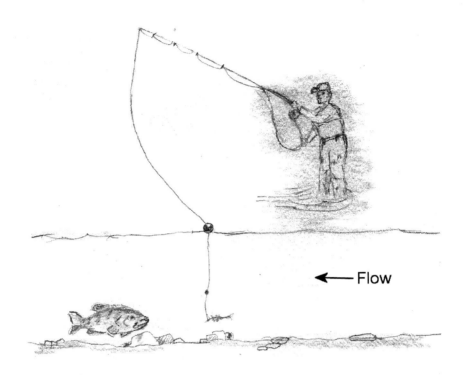

Flow

When using an indicator, never assume that a pause isn't a fish. It could be a snag but maybe not so lift with every change. The amount of line under the indicator has to be adjusted to suit the water depth so the fly is just off the bottom. Keep in mind that the water is moving slower near the bottom than on the surface.

The size and the type of the line or tippet are always important in all aspects of fly fishing. With nymphing it is common to use as heavy a tippet as possible without hampering the action of the fly. Heavier tippets hold up better to abrasion from rocks and the occasional snag. For smallmouth fishing a 3x tippet is usually sufficient, 2x for heavy, fast water especially if there are a lot of obstructions. Keep in mind that there are a lot of different brands on the market and they will vary so you may have to adjust for the brand that you are using. Smallmouth, basically, have the same food base as trout. And their feeding activity can be similar except that smallmouth are normally more aggressive and can therefore be less cautious. Still, at times, they can be just as wary as trout which may require changing to a lighter tippet. Sometimes going to just one size lighter will make a difference and get the fish going. I rarely have to go smaller than 4x for smallmouth unless maybe if they are feeding on midges or a small version of a Blue Winged olive.

Without definite current seams, the fish can be anywhere.

When working a section of river I don't overlook any of the water, especially if the conditions are right. If the conditions are good, smallmouth can be any where in the system. Even a small depression in the bottom may hold fish! The larger fish, however, are usually around the structure.

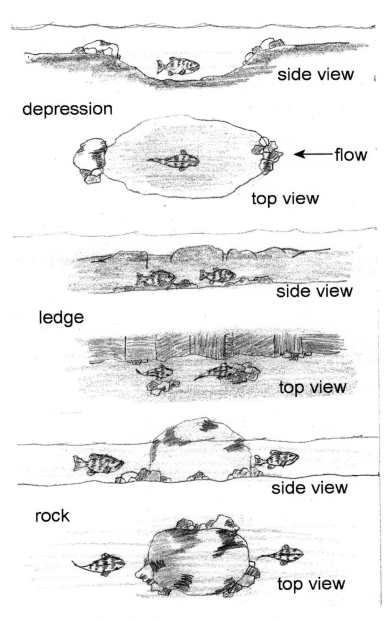

side view

depression

←flow

top view

side view

ledge

top view

side view

rock

top view

Typical types of stream structure

Rocks, either large or a group of smaller sizes, are ideal smallmouth habitat. Find the rocks in a river and you will invariably find the fish as well. In the case of large rocks, the fish will most likely be in front or in back of them where the current is less. You want to target these areas with your fly. Any underwater ledges or abrupt changes in depth are good holding areas. Move the fly out from the shallow water over the drop offs and in the case of streamers, let the fly fall down into the deeper water. A lot of times feeding fish will strike as soon as the fly begins to descend.

Trees that have fallen in the water, especially those that are creating current change, are fish magnets. This current change creates a current seam. Get on the side where the current is stronger if possible. This way you can dead drift the current with nymphs more effectively. Also, dropping a streamer just beyond the seam into the softer water and letting it swing out into the current can also work well. Always work these areas thoroughly regardless of weather you are fishing on top or under. Like most anglers, I like to catch fish on top whenever possible because it is exciting. If you are confident that the structure you are fishing holds fish but they won't come up, do not resist going under with a nymph or streamer. This tactic has produced many a fish for me that was reluctant to take off the top.

A weed bed should never be overlooked for smallmouth bass. Get the fly in as close as possible to the edge and let the fly sink for a couple of seconds before retrieving. Sometimes it's best to just let the fly swing out with the current and sometimes its good to impart some additional action by twitching, jigging, or stripping.

One of the desirable smallmouth traits, they flourish in urban waters.

If you come to a pool the fish will usually be at one end or the other. These are commonly referred to as the head or the tail of the pool. A pool is a body of slower water between two faster areas. The smaller fish tend to stay away from the larger ones so catching a smaller fish in the tail of the pool might mean that any bigger fish will be at the head. This is especially true if there is structure at either end. As stated, the structure might create a feeding lane where the current is directed or channeled for awhile. Any food items in that area of the stream will be swept down through that feeding lane. Feeding lanes are where the fish will be when they are active and feeding. They choose to hold in these in these lanes because the food items will come to them with the current. The biggest fish in this area will have what is called the best lie. The best lie is the best position to intercept the food. There is a "pecking" order with the next biggest fish being in the second best lie and so on.

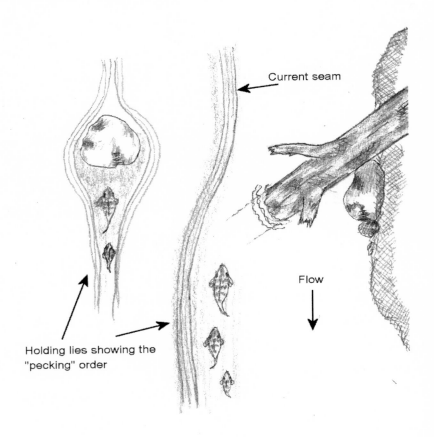

Current seam

Flow

Holding lies showing the "pecking" order

As you prepare to fish these lies, remember that your first pass through is the optimum chance at these fish so make it a good one. If you are not comfortable with the presentation, try something different. Change your position, the fly pattern, and the depth of the fly if you are fishing under or maybe a little less or more line. Almost always there are more fish in front of you than you realize so stay with this water until you are convinced that you do not have the right combination to attract these fish.

During the warmer months when fishing top water is the norm, pools are an excellent place to try surface patterns such as poppers and foam flies. There is such a variety of patterns available that I have no doubt you can find some that will work well on the water that you fish. If you are a tier, tying foam flies can be very enjoyable. They are relatively simple, easy to tie and you can really get creative with the patterns. It's a lot of fun to tie a new fly, try it out on the water, and catch a fish with it! If you have not tried your hand at tying, you should. It adds another dimension to the art of fly fishing. Catching a fish on one of your flies is very enjoyable and satisfying. Smallmouth will usually cooperate; this is one of their traits that make them such a wonderful game fish.

Foam can be used to imitate just about any insect and, of course, its floatability goes without saying. Smallmouth love foam flies! If there is sufficient current to keep the fly moving, I will always fish them dead drift. If you are having trouble dead drifting mend or loop the line upstream. This will prevent the line from pulling on the fly and keep the float drag free. This is an application for mending while fishing top water. Unlike poppers, foam flies do not need a lot of movement for them to be effective; however, some "twitching" at times can induce strikes. Tossing a foam fly back under some low hanging vegetation against the bank will usually bring an immediate take. If not, don't hesitate to twitch it out of there. A lot of times the larger fish will take the fly as soon as it hits the water but not always so stay with the retrieve to the end.

Another good method when fishing out in the middle of the stream where there is some current is to cast downstream with slack in the line. When the slack drifts out, wait a while, letting the fly hang in the current and giving it an occasional twitch. This works well in a river section where the current is not so strong and distributed across the width of the stream. With this water the fish can be anywhere in the system. When the current is in one area of the stream, the fish will be in the seam where the fast water and the slower water meet.

"Ringing the dinner bell" is a term that I read many years ago and still holds true today. This means splatting the fly down on the water to create a commotion and draw some interest from any fish in the area. There are times when a more subtle approach is better. Perhaps the latter should be tried first but you want to experiment with both ways. The successful angler will find the correct approach in order to catch fish. For example; there is a section of my home river that I have fished for many years. Year after year I will catch fish in the same areas using the same flies. But if one of those times the proven patterns and techniques don't work, I would not hesitate to try something different! Never assume that the fish are not there. Being flexible with your approach, methods and flies is crucial for continued success as you pursue the smallmouth bass.

Stream notes; when fishing a foam bug on the surface, drop it into the target area and let it sit for awhile. If there is a current, let it drift a ways without any induced movement. Unlike gills, smallmouths don't always need movement.

The key to catching fish with foam flies is to get them in to where the fish are holding, usually around some form of cover. Get the fly in as close as possible. The biggest smallmouth that I have caught was so tight to the cover that they only took when the fly bounced off the cover and plopped in the water! Smallmouth love rocks but their second choice is wood. You gotta get that fly in there and remember the first cast is your best shot at getting the larger fish.

Poppers are one of the more celebrated bass flies for top water and rightfully so, they are very effective and a lot of fun to fish with. Some form of popper may have been among the first surface flies developed to catch fish on top. There are a lot of different looks for poppers but they all have basically cylindrical bodies with either a flat or cupped out face that creates a "pop" when retrieved. This disturbance is what gets the attention of the fish. Smallmouth really like top water flies because they get a lot of their food off the surface, especially during the warmer months. Poppers also come with square or rectangular bodies that really move some water when stripped. By far the cylindrical bodies are most popular with anglers today. Back in the day, popper bodies were made from either cork or wood. These worked well for many years and are still available today. Modern poppers are mostly made from synthetic materials such as foam or plastic.

Popper fishing is exciting because you can see the strikes and the strikes are generally pretty aggressive. When fishing poppers, a good practice is to cast it out and let it sit for a while. Smallmouth will sometimes take a popper as it drifts naturally or sits quietly. As you start the retrieve, make short strips letting the fly rest a little between strips. An angler has to find the right tempo for the retrieve. The distance of the strip and the amount of time between the strips is important. Smallmouths seem to like a rhythmic retrieve. Different poppers and flies may require different retrieves so experiment until you find the right combination.

If you make your own poppers, try adding some rubber legs to increase the action of the fly, smallmouth love that leg movement. In terms of size, try larger poppers in the spring and early summer, up to size six. As the water warms, go down to a size ten. Color is another factor to consider. Just changing the color in the same pattern can generate some interest.

Stream notes; If possible, shave a flat on the bottom of the popper body. This will allow the fly to sit lower and "pop" better.

One of my favorites is the pencil popper. Pencil poppers are intended to imitate a wounded minnow struggling on the surface. All predator fish will key in on this activity which is why pencil poppers are so effective. If you encounter minnows that are jumping or skipping out of the water they are being chased by a predator fish. This is an excellent time to use a pencil popper. These poppers, like all poppers, come in a multitude of colors. All of which can be effective, however, white and black are the two colors you should always have in your box.

All of these flies that we have discussed can work at any time of the day or night. A popular belief is that the best fishing is early in the morning or just before dark. These are, without doubt, productive periods to fish but I have found that smallmouth will feed actively all day long! This is particularly true if there is a hatch coming off during the day that the smallmouths have keyed in on. When you encounter this scenario, approach these fish as you would a trout. Get into a good casting position and with an appropriate fly, cast into the feeding lanes with a drag free drift. If your presentation is good with no results, try another suitable pattern until you have exhausted all the top water options. Can't get them to come up yet the feeding activity continues, they are probably taking the emergers just as they reach the surface. This might be an opportune time to go with a wet fly, preferably one that resembles this emerger that is coming off the water. Cast over and across and let the fly swing out into the current. The fish will take this activity as an insect swimming to the surface to hatch.

There may be a time when you are fishing a hatch past daylight and into the dark. This can be very exciting; I have caught some real nice smallmouth in this situation. The first hour after dark is the optimum time to get a big bass. The big boys are less wary after dark and will feed more aggressively. And the strikes, well they can be shattering. You must be cautious, however, not to wade after dark unless you are familiar with the water. Well, we have gone over a lot of technical information in this chapter. I hope it will increase you're perspective on smallmouth fishing as well as you're catch rate. When you are successful in hooking a fish, keep in mind that smallmouth have a pugnacious attitude. They will fight hard, usually jump a couple of times, and simply refuse to come in! This is a wonderful experience for the angler;

however, you must be aware that smallmouth will fight to the point of exhaustion. Play them for a reasonable amount of time, bring the fish in, and release it back into its environment. Catch and release will insure their survival and releasing spawning fish is even more important. A female must be returned to lay her eggs and once deposited; the males need to fertilize the eggs and guard them until they hatch. Without the protection of the males their chances for survival are dismal at best! It is crucial to release spawning bass! Take the breeders out of a river system and in a couple of years, the fishery will fade away.

Stream notes; you may encounter some water that looks perfect for holding smallmouth. There's a good current and no surface activity so a nymph seems like a good choice. The first cast is followed downstream, retrieved and cast again. After several drifts with no reaction, discouragement sets in and you think about moving. Don't, not yet! Most likely the fish are there but the fly is not approaching them correctly. Never assume that the fish aren't there! Before you move, change tactics, the fly, or the presentation by adding some weight to get the fly down. The fly has to tumble downstream over the rocks just like a natural would. Accomplish this and you will wonder where all the fish came from.

Chapter Six

PATTERNS

How many smallmouth fly patterns are there? More than can be listed here even if I knew of them. Quite a few, however, have found their way to the end of my leader and most have proven successful.

As a novice fly fisherman, like many others, I began by using the standard flies that were considered effective at the time. From the beginning, those flies were effective and became even more so as my skills improved! Most of these established patterns are well documented in the many fine books available on the subject. I still use and recommend these patterns today.

After learning to tie flies and with the passing of several seasons, I began to develop a few patterns of my own. Some of these patterns are shown in this chapter along with several from other anglers that have influenced me with their expertise.

Any fly fisherman that does not tie flies should give it a try. Catching fish is always enjoyable to be sure but having success with a newly developed fly just adds another level of excitement to the sport.

Unpacking the boats for the family float down the river.

I tend to be redundant about things that are important such as staying flexible with regards to trying new and different flies regularly. Experimenting with new flies is just a lot of fun, especially when you catch a fish on a fly that you tied. Man, what a satisfying experience!

I have a deep appreciation for those tiers that have the patience and the skill to tie beautifully realistic flies. Those that I develop tend to be quick and easy so you can fish them aggressively without loss being a concern.

The following group of patterns is among those that I have found to work consistently over a period of time. Some are new, some are spinoffs, and all are effective and easy to tie. Included along with the recipe and tying instructions is a brief strategy for fishing them. Again, don't hesitate to try new stuff, the design variations are limitless. These flies are listed here alphabetically and will appear in the same order on the pattern pages.

1. Bell Hop
2. Black and Blue
3. Black Beauty
4. Buzzer
5. Chubby Gurgler
6. Clark's Crayfish
7. Clark's Twitchin Minnow
8. Copper Leach
9. Day Cray
10. Earshot
11. Foundit
12. Green and Mean
13. Hi-Joglin-Jiggler
14. Humpback
15. Huron Maiden

16. Huron Maiden II
17. Lucy
18. Prowler
19. Raisenator
20. Rapper
21. River Beau
22. Silver Streak
23. Simple Leech
24. Sprinter
25. Stinger
26. Warm-N-Fuzzy
27. Wendat
28. Wiggle Pop
29. Wispy
30. Yellow Dog

Stream notes; if you find a section of the river where you are taking fish consistently, this is a good time to try new patterns. Be sure to keep all the variables the same so that the only difference is the fly.

BELL HOP

Hook: Mustad 3366, Size 6-12

Thread: Uni-thread, Size 6/0

Body: Closed Cell Foam, 2mm thick, 3/8 in. wide, and 3 in. long.

Legs: Four Rubber Legs, Round, Size Medium

Wing: Closed Cell Foam, 2mm thick, 3/8 in. wide, and 3 in. long.

Sight Indicator: Closed Cell Foam, 2mm thick, 1/16 in. wide

Tying Instructions:

- Cut a slit at the end of the body foam at the tie-in point and slide   over hook bend.
- When tying in body, create three segments.
- Tie in rubber legs, two per side, between first and second segments.
- Tie in wing and indicator at first and second segments.
- Trim front of wing even with the hook eye and back of wing slightly past hook bend.
- Try different color combinations and hook sizes.

Fishing Tips:

Allow fly to drift with current and jig lightly to add movement. When fished in slow water or lakes, use a combination of slow strips and jigs to create movement.

History:

The "Bell Hop" was designed to imitate hoppers and other terrestrials. It was named after the Bell road access point of the Huron River where it was first fished and the word "hopper". The combination created the name "Bell Hop".

BLACK AND BLUE

Hook: Mustad 3366A size 6

Thread: 6/0 Black

Body: Electric blue flashabou

Tail: Chartreuse marabou

Wing: Black Marabou

Tying Instructions:

- Wrap a thread base on the hook shank Just behind the hook eye,
- Tie in several strands of the flashabou that extend 1 ½ inches past the bend of the hook.
- Tie in a marabou plume at the tip of the feather and palmer forward four to six turns and tie off behind the hook eye.
- Wrap a good head, whip finish and cement.

Fishing Tips:

The movement and the blue in this fly can draw some savage strikes.

BLACK BEAUTY

Hook: 3366A Mustad, size 6

Thread: 6/0 Black

Weight: Lead wire (optional)

Body: Black crosscut rabbit strip

Tail: Black marabou over several strands of black flashabou

Underbody: Several strands of black krystal flash

Tying Instructions:

- To create the underbody, tie in the flashabou behind the hook eye and wrap down to the bend of the hook and tie off.
- Tie in a clump of marabou that extends 1 ½" past the hook bend.
- Tie in several strands of black krystal flash on top of the marabou. Trim the black krystal flash a little shorter than the marabou.
- Tie in the crosscut rabbit strip and wrap forward two or three times to the eye of the hook stroking the fur back as you wrap forward to keep it laying back.
- Wrap a good head, whip finish, and cement.
- There are no eyes on this fly; weight can be added to the shank under the materials if desired.

Fishing Tips:

This is an excellent Smallmouth fly any time of the season. It is hard to fish this wrong!

BUZZER

Hook: Mustad 3366A size 8

Thread: 6/0 Black

Eyes: Small brass

Tail: Black Holographic flashabou

Body: Black crosscut rabbit

Tying Instructions:

- Tie in the eyes at the middle of the hook shank.
- Tie in several strands of flashabou behind the eyes.
- Tie in the crosscut rabbit strip in front of the eyes and wrap two times in front of the eyes.
- Tie in a good head, whip finish and cement.

Fishing Tips:

This fly is best fished in and around cover in low, clear water.

CHUBBY GURGLER

Hook: Mustad 94840 size 8

Thread: 6/0 Green

Eyes: 1/16 inch black plastic

Body: Chartreuse estaz

Tail: Chartreuse marabou

Overbody: 2mm lime green foam

Legs: medium round rubber in fluorescent chartreuse

Tying Instructions:

- Tie in the marabou tail at the hook bend so it extends about ¾" past the bend.
- Cut a length of the foam 3/8 "wide and about 2 inches long.
- Taper one end of the foam and tie behind the hook eye.
- Wrap the foam down tightly back to the bend.
- Tie in the estaz at the hook bend and let hang.
- Tie in a set of legs on each side and in the middle of the hook shank.
- Wrap the estaz forward around the legs and tie off behind the hook eye.
- Pull the foam forward over the estaz and tie down behind the hook eye.
- Place the eyes on the tie in point and fold the foam over the eyes trapping them in place and tie down behind the eyes.
- Trim off the excess foam a little higher than the body in a circular shape.
- Whip finish and cement.

Fishing Tips:

This pattern can be tied in different colors and sizes to suit your fishing conditions. In larger sizes, big bass will come off the bottom in slightly deeper water. Fish this fly dead drift with an occasional twitch to move the legs or a pop allowing the broad head to gurgle.

CLARK'S CRAYFISH

Hook: Mustad 3366A, Size 6-12

Eyes: 1/8' dumbbell

Thread: 6/0 Tan

Body: Natural rabbit or tan cross strip, three wraps only for a sparse look

Legs: Orange rubber, two per side

Underwing or tail: A few strands of copper krystal flash

Tying Instructions:

- Tie in the eyes on top of the shank about 1/16 inch back from the eye of the hook. Attach the krystal flash and the legs behind the eye, leave long and trim later.
- The legs should lie back along the side of the hook.
- Remove the hook from the vise; pierce the rabbit strip with the fur angling back so that it extends ¾ to 1 inch past the bend of the hook.
- Replace the hook and wind the thread up to the eye.
- Wind the strip forward three times keeping the tail fur on top of the shank. Wrap the strip over and around the eyes and tie in the head.
- Whip finish and cement.
- Trim all the fur off the underside of the shank to the bend of the hook.
- Trim the flash and the legs so they are just a little longer than the fur.
- Paint the eyes black. If using plain tan rabbit, use a marker to add some stripes to the fur.

Fishing Tips:

Crayfish are the most active during the warmer months when the water conditions are low and clear. When wading, crayfish are kicked up and dart downstream fast. Fish this fly by casting slightly upstream across the bank and retrieve with short and quick strips.

CLARK'S TWITCHIN MINNOW

Hook: Mustad 3399, size 6

Thread: 6/0 White

Head: Gold bead

Body: Pearl estaz

Tail: White marabou and pearl krystal flash

Overwing: Pearl flashabou

Tying Instructions:

- Mash down the barb on the hook and slide the gold bead up to the hook eye.
- Tie in the marabou tail so that it extends 1 ¼ inches past the bend of the hook.
- Wrap the remainder of the marabou forward as tight as possible and tie off behind the bead.
- Tie in the krystal flash on both sides of the hook shank back to the end of the marabou.
- Tie in the estaz at the hook bend and wrap forward to the bead. As you wrap the estaz forward, pull back on the material with each succeeding wrap. This creates a full body.
- Tie in several strands of the flashabou on top of the hook and behind the bead extending about ½ inch past the marabou.
- Tie off right behind the bead, whip finish, and cement.

Fishing Tips:

Because this fly is easy to see in the water you may witness the strike. Fish this fly with short cast and retrieve with a twitching motion. For more excitement, cast short and strip back real fast, erratically moving the rod tip. This technique imitates a minnow escaping a predator and will cause aggressive strikes. Fish this fly with a heavier tippet to prevent break offs.

COPPER LEECH

Hook: 3366A Mustad, size 6

Thread: 6/0 Brown

Eyes: 1/8" lead dumbbell

Body: Copper flashabou

Underwing: Brown rams wool

Overwing: Brown rams wool

Tying Instructions:

- Tie in the eyes 1/8" behind the hook eye.
- Tie in the flashabou right behind the lead eyes.
- Tie in a small clump of rams' wool on the bottom of the hook shank and in front of the eyes, should be a little shorter than the top portion.
- On top of the hook shank, tie in a larger clump of the wool in front of the eyes.
- Wrap a tapered head, whip finish and cement.
- Trim the flashabou slightly longer than the ram's wool.

Fishing Tips:

The rams' wool has a translucent appearance in the water that smallmouth love. This combined with its enticing movement makes this fly very effective throughout the season. Drop this fly in around structure, especially rocks, and hold on!

DAY CRAY

Hook: Mustad 3366A size 6

Thread: Large dumbbell

Legs: Brown and Orange medium rubber

Eyes: 1/8 inch dumbell

Body: Rust rabbit strip (solid or barred)

Wing: Olive marabou

Tying Instructions:

- Tie in the eyes about 2/3 back on the hook shank, tie the eyes down with some cement on the wraps.
- Tie in two orange legs on each side of the hook shank in front of the eyes.
- Cut a section of rust rabbit strip longer than needed and trim one end into a point.
- Tie in the pointed end of the rust rabbit strip behind the hook eye and on the bottom of the hook shank.
- Split the end of the rust rabbit strip up to the hook bend to create the pinchers.
- Tie in one brown leg on each side of the hook shank in front the eyes.
- Tie in a clump of olive marabou on top and in front of the hook eye, the marabou should extend ¾ inch past the hook bend.
- Wrap a good head, whip finish, and cement.
- Trim the rust rabbit strip 1 inch past the hook bend.
- Trim the legs so they are ½ "shorter than the olive marabou.

Fishing Tips:

Fish this fly when the crayfish are active. Cast across the current and allow the fly to sink. Retrieve the fly slowly by jigging it to create a hopping motion.

EARSHOT

Hook: 3366A Mustad, size 6

Thread: 6/0 to match

Eyes: Dumbbell or 1/8 inch bead chain

Body: Magnum white rabbit strip

Wing: Marabou, white

Tying Instructions:

- Tie in the eyes 1/6 of an inch bend the hook eye with a few wraps.
- Apply cement over the threads and continue to tie in the eyes wrapping through the cement.
- Cut a piece of rabbit strip 1 ½" long and trim one end into a "Vee".
- From the "Vee" end of the strip, at a distance equal to the length of the hook shank, pierce a hole in the rabbit strip.
- Remove the hook from the vise and slide the rabbit strip over the hook shank at the pierced hole with the hide side facing up. Place the hook back in the vise.
- Tie in the "Vee" end just behind the hook eye on the bottom of the shank.
- Tie in a few strands of flashabou that matches the rabbit strip, Tie in the flashabou in front of the eyes and behind the eyes so the flashabou lies down along the hook shank.
- Tie in a clump of short marabou, a little longer than the hook, in front of the eyes.

Fishing Tips:

Fish this fly in a little deeper and slower water.

FOUND IT

Hook: 3366A Mustad, size 6

Thread: 6/0 Gray

Eyes: Jungle cock (real or imitation)

Body: White marabou

Collar: Red hackle

Underwing: Several strands of pearl flasabou

Overwing: Four light dun feathers

Back: Four strands of peacock herl

Tying Instructions:

- Tie in the white marabou at the hook bend.
- Tie in and wrap the red hackle behind the hook eye.
- Trim off the top and sides of the red hackle to create the collar on the bottom of the hook.
- Tie in the flashabou on top of the hook behind the collar, trim the flashabou a little longer than the marabou.
- Tie in two feathers per side as long as the flashabou.
- Tie in the peacock herl on top of the feathers.
- Tie in a jungle cock eye on each side of the hook behind the hook eye. Ensure they are flat and on the side.
- Wrap the head, whip finish and cement.
- Trim the peacock herl a little shorter then the feathers.

Fishing Tips:

This is a good generic streamer pattern that imitates several species of bait fish. This fly is best fished with short cast from the angler. Power casting this fly tends to tangle the feathers.

GREEN & MEAN

Hook: 3261 Mustad Aberdeen size 8

Thread: 6/0 Yellow

Body: 1/16 inch bright green foam

Legs: Green and yellow barred

Hackle: Grizzly, dyed green

Indicator: Yellow foam

Tying Instructions:

- Cut a piece of foam 3/16" wide and one inch long.
- Align the end of the foam with the hook eye and tie in the foam ¼" behind the hook eye to create the first segment leaving a ½" tail.
- Move the thread forward to the first segment tie in point and tie in a set of legs on both sides so that they form an "X". Ensure the "X" is created correctly to separate the legs so that they do not foul around the hook point.
- Tie in the hackle and make two to four wraps.
- Tie in a thin, short strip of yellow foam at the first tie in point for the indicator.
- Wrap a head, whip finish and cement.
- Trim the indicator to the desired length.
- Trim the ends of the body to create a rounded look.
- Trim the legs to the desired length.

Fishing Tips:

This is another good generic pattern that can be effective anytime.

HIGH JOGGLIN JIGGLER

Hook: Mustad 3399 size 4

Thread: 6/0 Black

Eyes: brass that take a prismatic insert

Body: Black krystal flash chenille

Legs: Medium round black rubber

Tail: Black marabou tied long

Wing: Purple holographic flashabou

Tying Instructions:

- At the bend of the hook, tie in the flashabou long
- Tie the marabou long, wrap the excess marabou forward and tie off near the eye.
- Tie in the eyes on top of the marabou about 1/8" back from the hook eye.
- Tie in the chenille at the hook bend and let hang.
- Tie in the first set of legs on each side.
- Move the thread forward to near the eye and tie in the second set of legs.
- Wrap the chenille forward and around the first and second sets of legs.
- Wrap the chenille over and under the eyes to build a slightly larger head.
- Whip finish and cement, trim the flashabou to the same length as the tail.

Fishing Tips:

This fly should be fished like a standard streamer.

Fishing History:

The originator of this fly was fishing with traditional tackle and having an exceptional day. When asked by fellow anglers in a boat several yards away what he was using, his father replied "a Hawaiian Wiggler". The anglers said thank you and promptly told all anglers in the area that they were using a "High Jogglin Jiggler".

HUMPBACK

Hook: Mustad 3366, Size 6-12

Thread: Uni-thread, Size 6/0

Tail: Deer tail with a few strands of crystal flash

Body: Estaz chenille

Legs: Rubber Legs, Round, Size Medium

Back: Closed Cell Foam, 2mm thick, 3/8 in. wide, and 3 in. long.

Tying Instructions:

- Try different color combinations and hook sizes.
- Tie in deer tail with a few strands of crystal flash.
- Tie in estaz chenille and back at back of the hook.
- Tie in rubber legs, two per side.
- Wrap estaz chenille forward and around rubber legs creating a "Vee" pattern in legs. Tie off behind the hook eye.
- Pull the back over and tie off behind the hook eye, leaving excess foam to create a head.
- Whip finish and apply a drop of head cement.
- Trim head to shape.

Fishing Tips:

Allow fly to drift with current and jig lightly to add movement. When fished in slow water or lakes, use a combination of slow strips and jigs to create movement.

HURON MAIDEN

Hook: Mustad 3261 Aberdeen size 8 or 10

Thread: 6/0 to match

Eyes: 1/16 black plastic

Body: 2mm foam

Legs: Medium round rubber, color to match the body

Hackle: Stiff, color to match the body color

Tying Instructions:

- Cut a length of foam 1 ½ inches long that tapers from 1/16" at one end to 3/16" at the other end cutting a small "Vee" notch at the larger end.
- Tie in the large end of the foam behind the hook eye so 3/8" extends over the hook eye.
- Place the eyes on the tie in point and fold the foam over the eyes trapping them in place and secure with a couple soft wraps.
- Continue to tie in the foam at the same tie in point so the foam will extend up about 1/8 inch.
- Move the thread back ¼ inch to the second tie in point and tie in the legs.
- Tie in the hackle and make two to four wraps.
- Move the thread forward to the first tie in point.
- Tie in the second hackle and make two to four wraps. Ensure the plastic eyes are secure as you move forward with several wraps of thread between the foam and the eye of the hook.
- Trim legs to desired length, whip finish and cement.

Fishing Tips:

A good pattern when either damsels or hex flies are on the water. Fish like a dry fly, dead drift with no drag. I have found dull green, blue, black and yellow to be effective color.

HURON MAIDEN II

Hook: Mustad 3261 Aberdeen size 4 or 6

Thread: 6/0 to match

Eyes: 1/16 black plastic

Hackle: Stiff, color to match the body color

Body: 2mm foam

Legs: Medium round rubber, color to match the body

Tying Instructions:

- Cut a length of foam 1 ½ inches long that tapers from 1/16" at one end to 3/16" at the other end cutting a small "Vee" notch at the larger end.
- Tie in the large end of the foam behind the hook eye so 3/8" extends over the hook eye.
- Place the eyes on the tie in point and fold the foam over the eyes trapping them in place and tie in the foam at the same tie in point so the foam will extend up about 1/8 inch.
- Tie in three ¼ inch segments to create the body, advance the thread back to the first tie in point.
- Tie in the legs and the hackle making two to four wraps of hackle.
- Trim legs to desired length.
- Whip finish and cement.

Fishing Tips:

This fly is deadly when hexes are on the water. Fishing dead drift or with a twitch are equally effective. If you see smallmouth rising to hexes, cast the fly in the ring of the rise as soon as possible and this will initiate a strike. Brown and tan are effective colors.

LUCY

Hook: 3366A Mustad, size 6

Thread: 6/0 White

Eyes: 1/8' bead chain

Body: Opal mirage

Rib: Copper wire

Tail: Mirage flashabou

Wing: Marabou

Tying Instructions:

- Tie in the eyes 1/6 of an inch bend the hook eye.
- Tie in the copper wire behind the eyes and wrap to the hook bend.
- Tie in the opal mirage flashabou at the hook bend.
- Wrap the flashabou forward and tie down behind the eye.
- Wrap the copper wire forward to create a rib and tie off behind the eye.
- Tie in a few strands of opal mirage flashabou behind the eye, trim later.
- Strip the fibers from the bottom of the marabou plume shaft and ½ inch from the tip of the marabou plume and tie in front of the eyes.
- Wrap the marabou around the hook shank 6 times in front of the eyes taking care not to break the plume and stroke the fibers back with every wrap.
- Wrap head large enough to keep the fibers laying back, whip finish and cement.

Fishing Tips:

Fishing this fly is exciting as it will elicit some savage strikes! The slim profile and translucent look is real attractive to predator fish.

PROWLER

Hook: Mustad 79580, size 6 or 8

Eyes: 3/16' dumbbell

Tail: Black marabou tied fairly heavy

Body: Large black Estaz

Legs: Black rubber left long, two per side

Wing: Black marabou tied in at the tip

Thread: 6/0 Black

Tying Instructions:

- Attach the eyes on top of the shank.
- Tie in the marabou tail.
- Tie in the estaz at the bend and wind forward to the eyes.
- Attach two legs per side at this point.
- Tie in the marabou by the tip in front of the eyes and wrap a few times.
- Stroke back the plumes with each wrap.
- Tie a substantial head so that the marabou lays back.
- Whip finish and cement.

Fishing Tips:

The prowler can be very effective in the spring, just use conventional streamer techniques.

RAISENATOR

Hook: Mustad 3366A size 6
Thread: 6/0 Brown
Eyes: Red dumbbell
Body: rust magnum rabbit strip
Wing: Olive marabou

Tying Instructions:

- Tie in the eyes 1/8" behind the hook eye.
- Cut a length of the rabbit strip 1 ½ inches long and trim one end into a point.
- Tie in the point of the rabbit strip on the hook bottom just in front of the eyes.
- Split the end of the rabbit strip up to the hook bend to create the pinchers.
- Tie in a clump of marabou on top of the hook in front of the eyes.
- Wrap a nice head, whip finish and cement.

Fishing Tips:

This pattern works best when the crayfish are active.

RAPPER

Hook: Mustad 3261 Aberdeen size 8 or 6

Thread: 6/0 Black

Legs: Medium black or centipede

Body: 2mm black foam

Sight Indicator: 2mm yellow (optional)

Tying Instructions:

- Wrap the entire length of the hook shank with thread to create a good base.
- Cut a piece of foam 3/16 inch wide and 1 inch long.
- Position the foam even with the hook eye and tie in the foam securely 5/16 inch behind the eye to create the first tie in point.
- Move the thread back ¼ inch for the second tie down point and tie in the foam.
- Tie in a black hackle, wrap three times and tie off.
- Move the thread to the first tie down point and tie in two legs on both sides of the foam so they stick out from the body at least ¾ inch.
- Tie in a black hackle, wrap three times and tie off.
- Optional, tie in a short piece of yellow foam on top of the hackle and cinch down.
- Move the thread forward and whip finish under the head section.
- Cement the tie down points and the thread tie off point.
- Trim the corners off the foam to give it a rounded buggy look.

Fishing Tips:

This fly works great for panfish as well as smallies.

RIVER BEAU

Hook: Mustad 79580 3x, size 6 or 8

Eyes: Silver or gold 1/8 bead chain

Thread: 6/0 in any green shade

Body: Medium chenille in chartreuse

Hackle: Soft hackle in chartreuse tied long

Rib: Gold or copper wire

Tail: Chartreuse marabou with a few strands of pearl krystal flash

Tying Instructions:

- Tie in the eyes 1/6 of an inch bend the hook eye.
- Tie in a clump of marabou at the bend of the hook. Include a few strands of pearl or green krystal flash.
- Tie in a length of copper wire at the bend of the hook.
- Tie in the chartreuse chenille and hackle at the bend of the hook.
- Wrap the chartreuse chenille forward crisscrossing over and under the eyes, tying off behind the hook eye.
- Palmer the hackle forward followed by the copper wire rib and tie both off just behind the hook eye.
- Whip finish and cement.

Fishing Tips:

What this fly looks like to a bass I don't know but it rarely fails to catch fish.

SILVER STREAK

Hook: Mustad 3366A, size 6

Eyes: Silver bead chain, 3/16 diameter

Thread: 6/0 White

Body: White crosscut rabbit strip

Tail: Several strands of pearl or Mirage opal flashabou over white marabou

Tying Instructions:

- Starting at the bend, tie in a clump of white marabou, I prefer Blood Quill Marabou, especially for the tails. The plumes are a little thicker.
- Attach the flashabou over the tail and let it extend just beyond the marabou.
- Tie in the eyes 1/6 of an inch bend the hook eye with a few wraps.
- Apply cement over the threads and continue to tie in the eyes wrapping through the cement.
- Tie in the crosscut rabbit strip near the bend of the hook and wrap forward two or three times depending on the thickness of the strip.
- Bring the last wrap behind the eyes up and forward between the eyes and around the hook shank twice. It gets a little crowded but when the head is tied in, it will lay the fur back over the eyes for a natural look.
- Whip finish and cement.

Fishing Tips:

When retrieving this fly, "pop" it as though it were on the surface. This gives it a struggling motion under the water.

SIMPLE LEECH

Hook: 3366A Mustad, size 6

Thread: 6/0 Brown

Body: Magnum dark brown rabbit strip

Tying Instructions:

- Tie in a length of rabbit strip two times the length of the hook shank behind the hook eye.
- Wrap a nice head, whip finish, and cement. That's it!

Fishing Tips:

This fly works well in the spring and early summer. Add weight as needed to get the fly close to the bottom. Retrieve with short strips allowing the fly to drop down and swim back up to imitate a leech's movement.

SPRINTER

Hook: 3366A Mustad, size 6

Thread: 6/0 White

Body: A single wrap of Opal Mirage

Underbody: Pearl krystal flash tied short, just past the rabbit

Overbody: White crosscut rabbit strip

Tail: Several strands of pearl flashabou

Tying Instructions:

- Wrap the shank with the opal mirage flashabou and tie off behind the hook eye.
- Tie in the pearl flashabou just behind the hook eye extending at least one inch past the bend of the hook.
- Tie in the pearl krystal flash on top of the pearl flashabou. This will be trimmed later.
- Tie in the rabbit strip about halfway down the shank. Wrap twice and tie off just behind the hook eye.
- Wrap a good head, whip finish, and cement.
- Trim the krystal flash so that it is just longer than the rabbit strip.

Fishing Tips:

Fishing this pattern with a lot of movement and a jiggle retrieve is very deadly.

STINGER

Hook: Mustad Aberdeen 2x size 10

Thread: 6/0 Black

Legs: Medium black and white rubber

Body: 3mm foam black

Sight Indicator: 3mm foam yellow

Tying Instructions:

- Cut a piece of foam 3/16" wide and one inch long.
- Align the end of the foam with the hook eye and tie in the foam ¼" behind the hook eye to create the first segment.
- Move the thread back and tie in the foam ¼" to make the second segment leaving a ½" tail.
- Move the thread forward to the first segment tie in point and tie in a set of legs on both sides so that they form an "X". Ensure the "X" is created correctly to separate the legs so that they do not foul around the hook point.
- Tie in a thin, short strip of yellow foam at the first tie in point for the indicator.
- Wrap a head, whip finish and cement.
- Trim the indicator to your desired length.
- Trim the ends of the body to create a rounded look.
- Trim the legs to the desired length.

Fishing Tips:

Fish this fly like a dry fly, dead drift with the current. An excellent pattern if there are any insects on the water. This is an excellent ant imitation tied in smaller sizes.

WARM-N-FUZZY

Hook: Mustad 9171 or any standard nymph hook, size 10 or 12

Bead: 1/8' copper or brass

Thread: 6/0 Brown

Body: Light hares ear dubbing

Rib: Lighter copper wire

Tail: Rabbit guard hairs

Tying Instructions:

- Mash the barb down on the hook to slide the bead on.
- Attach the thread and wind back to the bend.
- Select a small clump of rabbit fur, remove the under fur so that all you have left are the guard hairs.
- Attach these so that they extend a little past the bend of the hook.
- Tie in a length of light copper wire.
- Begin dubbing at the tail and move forward increasing the body size as you go. Tie off the dubbing behind the bead. Wind the rib forward, tie off behind the bead.
- Add a little more loose dubbing and sink a couple of half hitches down behind the bead It may not be necessary but I like to cement the head, in this case, very sparingly.

Fishing Tips:

This is a 'go to' fly for Smallies. It is most effective when the fishing is slow. Cast into the bank and let it swing out or dead drift it down with the current. When dead drifting add enough weight to get the fly near the bottom.

WENDAT

Hook: Mustad 3261 Aberdeen size 8 or 10

Thread: 6/0 Tan

Body: 2 mm foam, 1' long

Legs: Medium round rubber, barred to match the color of the body.

Hackle: Stiff brown (optional)

Wing: Natural deer hair

Tying Instructions:

- Tie in the 1 inch piece of foam behind the hook eye to create the first ¼" segment.
- If using hackle, tie in, wrap two to four turns and tie off.
- Move the thread back and tie in the second ¼" segment leaving a ½" tail.
- If using hackle, tie in, wrap two to four turns and tie off.
- Advance the thread forward to the first segment and tie in the legs on both sides.
- Clean, trim, and stack a clump of deer hair.
- Tie in the deer hair so that it is slightly shorter then the body.
- Wrap a head under the first section of foam, whip finish and cement.
- Trim the flared deer hair to the desired length.
- Trim the legs to the desired length.

Fishing Tips:

A good late summer fly. Body colors of yellow, tan and brown are all effective.

Fly History:

During the exploration of Michigan by the French. A tribe of Indians living near the Detroit River in the area which is now the city of Wyandotte were named Wendats. The Detroit and Huron rivers were an integral part of this tribe's lifestyle and culture. This fly was developed and first fished on the Huron River and named for this tribe.

WIGGLE POP

Hook: Mustad light wire 3261 Aberdeen, size 6

Thread: 6/0 white

Body: 1/4' diameter foam, cut to 20mm long with the face at a slight angle

Hackle: optional, use a suitable popper hackle in a matching color

Tail: A short length of magnum rabbit strip a suitable color

Tying Instructions:

- Bend the eye of the hook down at a 45 degree angle so that it will extend below the foam body.
- Slit the foam and glue on the hook so that there is a 3mm gap between the eye and the face of the foam body. Ensure that there is adequate shank length behind the foam body to attach the materials.
- Tie in the rabbit strip securely. You may chose to include some hackle in a suitable color, if so, wrap the hackle over where the rabbit is tied in.
- Whip finish and cement.

Fishing Tips:

This fly will work all season especially when the bass are chasing minnows. Cast it back into soft water, let it sit for about five seconds. Make the strips short but firm, this will generate the wiggle movement.

WISPY

Hook: Mustad 3366A size 8

Thread: 6/0 White

Eyes: Medium size hourglass in silver

Body: Opal mirage flashabou

Tail: Opal mirage flashabou

Collar: White rams wool

Wing: White rams wool

Tying Instructions:

- Tie in the eyes ¼" behind the hook eye.
- Tie in a single strand of opal mirage flashabou behind the eyes and wrap to the hook bend and back to create a body.
- Tie in several strands of opal mirage flashabou behind the eyes extending 1 ½ inches past the bend of the hook.
- Tie in a small clump of rams' wool on the hook bottom and in front of the eyes stretching a little past the hook bend.
- Tie in a larger clump of rams' wool on top of the hook and in front of the eyes as long as the material allows but no longer than the opal mirage flashabou.
- Wrap a good head, whip finish and cement.

Fishing Tips:

This pattern has a very slim profile with a lot of flash. When this fly is retrieved, twitching it erratically almost always draws a strike.

YELLOW DOG

Hook: Mustad 3261 Aberdeen size 6 or 8

Thread: 6/0 Yellow

Legs: Round yellow, two per side tied in along the center section

Body: 2 mm thick yellow foam tied into three sections

Tying Instructions:

- Wrap the entire length of the hook shank with thread to create a good base.
- Cut a piece of foam 3/16 inch wide and 1 3/16 inches long.
- Position the foam even with the hook eye and tie in the foam securely 5/16 inch behind the eye to create the first tie in point.
- Move the thread back ¼ inch for the second tie down point and tie in the foam.
- Move the thread back ¼ inch for the third tie down point and tie in the foam.
- Move the thread forward ¼ inch to the second tie down point and tie in two legs on both sides of the foam so they stick out from the body at least ¾ inch. .
- Pull the legs up and tie down on both sides. This will keep the legs separated. Trim the legs to the desired length.
- Move the thread forward ¼ inch to the first tie down point and whip finish behind the eye on the hook shank.
- Cement the tie down points and the thread tie off point. I usually trim the corners off the foam to give it a rounded buggy look.

Fishing Tips:

Cast this fly close to cover and wait. If no action, retrieve with slow strips, still no response, intensify the strips pausing in between.

116

The Last Cast

Well, here we are taking one more cast, the last one for now. I sure hope the material that we covered in these chapters will be a useful tool. It was mentioned early on about having good equipment. Fishing for smallmouth does not require real sophisticated gear; however, improving the equipment will just add more enjoyment to the sport. My opinion, buy the best gear that suits you're needs and you're budget. Seek out the advice of seasoned anglers before choosing, they have probably been through the experimenting cycle already. Of course, using good equipment improves our chances for catching fish but what really matters is our attitude towards fly fishing and how well we apply what we know on the stream.

Sharing information with other anglers creates a friendly environment, perhaps just as significant as any technical data that was exchanged. I will never understand those anglers that feel the fly they are using with success is the last secret of the universe! Many friendships, some long term, began with the simple exchange of a fly on the stream.

Showing respect for the sport, the fish, and other anglers is a trait we should all have and if not, need to acquire. It is essential for us to pass this on to beginning fly fishermen, regardless of their age.

Learn all you can about smallmouth bass. The more that you do, the easier it will be to locate and catch them. Smallmouths are fairly predictable, especially in rivers that don't change much from one year to the next. A prime lie that remains intact will always hold fish.

The techniques discussed in chapter five are the meat and potatoes of this narrative. It is, after all, how well these strategies are applied that will determine the number of fish caught. It's always enjoyable to be on the river but, let's face it, its more fun when you're catching fish.

Are there truly any new fly patterns? Probably, but most of the flies that I tie are just variations of existing patterns. Not that there is anything wrong with this. Many times I have modified a fly, sometimes just a subtle change, and it becomes more effective. Some of the patterns that are included here may seem similar but there are differences that have proven to be successful. Experimenting with new flies is an aspect of the sport that I truly love. It falls in line with the flexible attitude noted throughout this book. Flexibility and adjustment are key factors for effective smallmouth fishing or any fishing for that matter. An angler may have to make adjustments continually through the day, not easy to do, but necessary to meet the changing conditions. Addressing these changes is the way to catch more smallmouth bass.

So good luck pursuing the intrepid smallmouth bass and I hope all your days on the river are memorable ones.

Appendix A

Visual information

CHAPTER ONE

Photograph of a smallmouth bass

Distribution map showing the range of smallmouth

CHAPTER TWO

One of my streamer fly boxes

CHAPTER THREE

Photographs comparing a smallmouth and a largemouth

Pattern photos and recipes are listed alphabetically

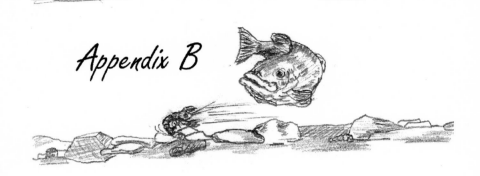

Appendix B

Contact information

MICHIGAN DNR - DEPARTMENT OF NATURAL RESOURCES FOR SOUTHERN MICHIGAN

Fisheries............................517-373-1280

Parks & Recreation...............517-373-9900

Southfield Service Center.......248-359-9040

Weekly fishing report.............517-373-0908

FLY FISHING SHOPS IN SOUTH EAST MICHIGAN

The Orvis Store....................248-542-5700

Hanks Fly Fishing Unlimited...248-393-1500

Bass Pro Shops...................248-209-4200

Colton Bay Outfitters.............734-222-9776

BAIT AND TACKLE SHOPS IN SOUTH EAST MICHIGAN

Little Dipper.........................734-782-4277

Bottom Line.........................734-379-9762

Bait and Tackle Box..............734-675-5662

Trenton Lighthouse...............734-675-7080

Jeff's Bait and Tackle.............734-289-4901

AREA RETAIL STORES WITH FISHING SUPPLIES

Cabelas.............................734-529-4700

Gander Mountain...................734-287-7420

Dick's................................734-374-0429

Dunhams............................734-479-1300

CANOE LIVERIES IN THE AREA

Argo-Gallup Park...................734-662-9319

River Raisen........................734-529-9029

Heavener............................248-437-9406

Sawmill tube and Canoe..........231-796-6408

AREA METROPARKS – ALL OFFER FISHING ACCESS

Delhi Metropark

Local................................734-426-8211

Outside........................1-800-477-3191

Dexter – Huron Metropark

Local................................734-426-8211

Outside........................1-800-477-3191

Hudson Mills Metropark

Local................................734-426-8211

Outside........................1-800-477-3191

Huron Meadows Metropark

Local................................734-426-8211

Outside........................1-800-477-3191

Lower Huron Metropark

Local................................734-697-9181

Outside........................1-800-477-3182

Kensington Metropark

Local................................248-685-1561

Outside........................1-800-477-3178

Lake Erie Metropark

Local................................734-379-5020

Outside........................1-800-477-3189

Oakwood's Metropark

Local................................734-782-3956

Outside........................1-800-477-3182

Willow Metropark

Local................................734-697-9181

Outside........................1-800-477-3182

Bibliography

John Whitlock, "Micropterus museum of Zoology, 2004

William Fink (editor, instructor), University of Michigan

Tim Holschalag, Smallmouth Fly Fishing, The best Techniques, Flies, and Destinations – Smallmouth Angler Press, 2005

Lefty Kreh, Fly Fishing for Bass-The Lyons Press, 2004

Dirk Fishbach, The Fly Fisher's Huron – Dirk Fishbach, 2001

Joe Bruce, Fly Fishing for Smallmouth Bass – K&D Limited, Inc., 1997

Dan Sura, Dave Csanda, Bob Ripley, Ron and Al Linder, Doug Strange, Larry Dalhberg, Smallmouth Bass An In Fisherman handbook of strategies – Al Linder's Outdoors, Inc.,1995dolomieu: Information".

Animal diversity web
. Ann Arbor: University of Michigan M

Charles Waterman, Black Bass and the Fly Rod – Stackpole, 1993

Pam Fuller. 2010. Micropterus dolomieu. USGS Nonindigenous Aquatic Species Database, Gainesville, Fl.

Will Ryan, Smallmouth Strategies for the Fly Rod – Lyons and Burford, 1996

Harry Murray, Fly Fishing for Smallmouth Bass – Lyons and Burford publishers, 31 West 21 Street, New York, NY 10010, 1989

A.J. McClane, McClane's Field Guide to Freshwater Fishes of North America – Holt, Rinchart, and Winston, Inc., 1974

James Henshall, Book of the Black Bass – Robert Clarke & Co., Cincinnati, 1881

Orvis fly fishing schools online handbook.

Various issues of the following magazines from 2000 to 2010; In Fisherman, Field and Stream, Fly Fisherman, American Angler, Warm Water Fishing, Fly Rod and Reel and Michigan Out of Doors.

Wikipedia, the free encyclopedia.

Index

NOTES

NOTES

NOTES